P9-DNB-030

TURN TOWARD THE WIND

TURN TOWARD THE WIND

EMBRACING CHANGE IN YOUR LIFE

DALE HANSON BOURKE

ZondervanPublishingHouse

Grand Rapids, Michigan

A Division of HarperCollins*Publishers*

E D I T I O N

Turn Toward the Wind
Copyright © 1995 by Dale Hanson Bourke

Requests for information should be addressed to:

ZondervanPublishingHouse
Grand Rapids, Michigan 49530

Library of Congress Cataloging-in-Publication Data

Bourke, Dale Hanson.
    Turn toward the wind : embracing change in your life / Dale Hanson Bourke.
       p.   cm.
    Includes bibliographical references.
    ISBN: 0–310–41170–X (alk. paper)
    1. Life change events—Religious aspects—Christianity. 2. Loss (Psychology)—
Religious apsects—Christianity. 3. Adjustment (Psychology)—Religious aspects—
Christianity. I. Title
BV4908.5.B68   1995
248.4—dc20   95–32869
                                                     CIP

This edition printed on acid-free paper and meets the American National Standards
Institute Z39.48 standard.

All Scripture quotations, unless otherwise indicated, are taken from the *Holy Bible: New
International Version®*. NIV®. Copyright © 1973, 1978, 1984 by International Bible
Society. Used by permission of Zondervan Publishing House. All rights reserved.

Published in association with the literary agency of Alive Communications, Colorado
Springs, CO 80949

Interior design by Susan Vandenberg-Koppenol

Printed in the United States of America

---

95 96 97 98 99 00 01 02 /❖DH/ 10 9 8 7 6 5 4 3 2 1

CONTENTS

ACKNOWLEDGMENTS

This is a book about the way God works in the lives of those who seek him. Because those of us who share our stories have tried to be honest, we have exposed some of the aspects of our lives we aren't always proud of.

I am grateful to "Jack" and others who allowed me to tell their stories. Most of their names have been changed and in some cases I have altered other details to disguise their identities. This was done only to protect their families and the others involved in their stories and in no way changes the details of how God was at work in their lives.

There are many people who have shared my own journey. I am grateful to them for their love, encouragement, and patience.

Kip Jordon, publisher of Word, is a dear friend, and it was during a conversation with him that the title of this book was born. Scott Bolinder, publisher of Zondervan, has lived through many changes personally and has encouraged me in both the living and the telling of my story. Bruce Barbour, publisher of Moorings, is yet another dear friend who helped me craft my words and prayed me through to the end. They may compete with one another, but I am fortunate to count each as my friend.

Rick Christian, my agent, has pushed me, comforted me, and patiently advised me in this and other adventures.

Laura Barker, friend and coworker, assisted in researching, editing, and providing constant encouragement.

Michelle Rapkin, Mary Hopkins Bailey, Roberta Croteau, Bonnie Keen, Sheila Walsh, Julie Talerico, Becky Pippert, Leslie Nunn, Holly Townsend, Nancy Norris, Wendy Goldberg, Vickie Smick, Laura Minchew, and others have been friends and crafters of words and ideas. Each of them has given me an idea or added a concept to this book.

Sandy Vander Zicht and Lori Walburg have both done an exceptional job of pulling my random thoughts together into a book.

My "boys"—Tom, Chase, and Tyler—have given me space and time to work on this manuscript and, of course, have lived through the events with me. Thanks, guys.

And finally, I am grateful for the legacy from my grandmother and her son, my father, which is a treasured gift of love and hope in the face of change.

INTRODUCTION

I had known Jack for years, but I realized one day that I really didn't know him at all. At least I didn't know who he had become. I remember clearly who he had been when I had first met him ten years before. He was young, impatient, and self-assured. He had the world by the tail and didn't hesitate to let everyone know it. He was on a roll, and you could run along beside him or get left behind.

But life hadn't gone the way he'd planned. The company he worked for and hoped to run one day was sold. His marriage ended. His personal and professional lives crashed at the same time, and Jack was shattered.

We had worked together years before, and now I was considering doing some work for Jack again. But I was hesitant. He had been tough to work for in his younger days. I didn't want to deal with his impatience or his arrogance again.

So as I sat in a meeting with Jack and others, I was looking for signs of trouble. *He's on his best behavior*, I thought cynically, as I watched him interacting with others. Then a young woman spoke up hesitantly, trying to make a point. One man chuckled and began to speak over her, and she stopped what she was saying and turned red.

But then Jack spoke up. "I think Cathy is making a good point," he said, coming to her defense and giving her credibility in the group. "Tell us more," he said, turning the attention back to the grateful young woman.

I watched this interaction and others that day and knew that I had been wrong. Jack wasn't just acting. He wasn't on his best behavior; he had *changed* his behavior. He was more sensitive, more willing to listen, more aware of those around him. He was still Jack— outgoing, funny, bold—but he was profoundly different from the man I had known before.

Toward the end of the meeting someone mentioned a story he had read about miracles. Some people said they believed in miracles; others rolled their eyes and joked. I just looked at Jack.

Later we sat at lunch and Jack asked me what I had thought of the discussion. I tried to find the words to express what I had realized that morning. "I've never actually seen a *physical* miracle," I explained. "I've never seen a lame person suddenly walk or a blind man who could now see.

"But I do think I witnessed a miracle this morning. I have seen what God has done in your life, Jack. If he could change you as profoundly as he has, I can't help but believe in physical healings, too."

Jack and I spent the rest of lunch reminiscing about the "old days" and talking about the painful times he had gone through. He told me how the difficulties had sent him to his knees in despair and how God had become more and more real to him. We both had tears in our eyes as we realized that we had been on separate but parallel journeys. God had changed each of us in profound ways. Each of us had felt hurricanes tear through our lives, uprooting all we held dear. Unable to cope, we had simply given up. And in giving up our own wills, we had allowed God to mold us in ways we could never have imagined.

BEYOND COPING

The challenge to those of us who want to follow God is to go beyond the human response to change, which at its best is coping, and move to the divine process, which in Greek is called *metanoia*, or a moving from what is old to what is new. Coping is done on the same level that we live our daily lives. But true change, true biblical *metanoia*, is a spiritual change that gives us new insight and outlook. To experience that type of change requires going beyond pop psychology and into a realm which most of the world—and much of the church itself—does not understand. It means giving up what we actually know for what we know exists only through faith. It involves moving from what is seen to what is unseen.

For the seeker, times of crisis become moments of insight or insulation, a time to move closer to God as he truly is or a time to stubbornly hold on to our image of him. As Madeleine L'Engle noted in her book *Walking on Water*, "The Jesus we grasp and the Jesus who grasps us may differ."

Change is always a death of something we have held closely for a time and a beginning of something unseen, untested, or unknown. Chaim Potok started a novel aptly titled *In the Beginning* by quoting a line of the ancient Jewish Midrash: "All beginnings are hard." Change hurts, even when we choose it. It is frightening, even when we boldly push forward. It undoes us, and we never know what we will be like when the pieces are put back together again.

Change hurts, even when we choose it.

When I was a young girl, our Sunday night church services always included a time of testimonies. Too often these were times when people got up and praised God for some wonderful event that had happened. There is nothing wrong with that, of course, but I grew up with a sense that I was the only one who was muddling through. Week after week I looked for something wonderful enough to tell about during testimony time.

Then one night a young woman stood up tentatively and spoke as well as she could through her sobs. I don't remember her exact circumstances, but they were tragic and seemed to be getting worse. She ended her testimony with the words, "I'm still trying to trust God—but it isn't easy."

Hers is the only testimony that remains real to me today. The rest are a sea of smiling faces and booming voices that told me if only I had enough faith, God would make everything all right. I know now that many of those people were probably suffering behind their masks. And now I realize that the young woman who embarrassed many of the more proper members of our church was more open to God than those who could cite verse upon verse and phrase everything the right way. But I wish more people had stood and spoken out of despair. I wish that as a child I had understood that the Bible does not contain the phrase, "And they all lived happily ever after."

IT DON'T COME EASY

Many of us are not living happily ever after. And yet those of us who believe in God are living with the knowledge that what comes after life is worth waiting for. When changes come into our lives—and they will—we can resist them and at best learn to cope, or we can celebrate them and ask God to use the circumstances to change us in deeper ways.

The Bible does not contain the phrase, "And they all lived happily ever after."

⤞   ⤝

What the people in this book have in common is that they have, sometimes through clenched teeth, asked God to change them. And even though they have experienced pain, heartbreak, and disappointment, not one of them would go back to the way they were before they were broken. Every one of them has learned that there is more to life than coping. Once they had emerged from their dark tunnels of fear and sorrow, they could see that God was doing new things.

We may not even know we have changed until someone else notices. Or perhaps we do something that seems "natural" one day and realize that a few years before it would have been contrary to our instincts. Change takes time and effort and, at first, a conscious desire to want to change and practice new behaviors.

One day I was pouring my heart out to a friend I'll call Gail. Suddenly I stopped and thanked her for being the kind of person I could trust. Although I had known her well for only a year, I felt she was a kindred spirit, someone with whom I could share my concerns.

She startled me by saying, "I didn't used to be this way." We talked about her own journey and the difficult path of going from someone who was self-absorbed and afraid of attachment to becoming someone who could invest herself in others. I had never known that she was any other way; she knew that the person she had become was not very much like the person she had been.

Gail and I took a moment to look back at how far she had come and to celebrate her success at having survived the painful journey. It gave us both hope that God would continue to work in our lives. And it strengthened our resolve to seek change, even when it is uncomfortable, because we know the results are worth the pain.

If life has seemed unfair at times, if things haven't worked out the way you planned, this book is for you. If you are a believer who sometimes wonders whether your beliefs make that much of a difference, come join us on the journey. If you like to hold on to things the way they are and dread the changes that interrupt your life, consider choosing a different way, one that relieves you of the stress of holding things tightly and controlling everything you can.

The Bible tells us that the truth will set us free, but it doesn't promise that it will be pleasant or easy.

In the following pages you will learn more about Jack and others who have allowed God to do a new thing in their lives. I share my own experiences and the stories of others not out of pride or because we have learned so much. In fact, many of the stories are of brokenness, humiliation, and pain. Often the "right choice" brings us face to face with grisly truth and painful decisions. The Bible tells us that the truth will set us free, but it doesn't promise that it will be pleasant or easy.

Most of the Christian life is learning to surrender and grow through circumstances that are not always clear or clean. Changing, really changing, is a road without signposts. Each day brings another opportunity to take a step on the journey of change. There are no signs and few mile markers.

God's promise to Isaiah still rings true today:

See, I am doing a new thing!
Now it springs up; do you not perceive it?
I am making a way in the desert
and streams in the wasteland. (Isa. 43:19)

God promises to do a new thing in each of us. He doesn't ask for anything more than our willingness to turn toward him and away from self, the openness to let the wind of his Spirit blow through our lives.

Part One

THE CHALLENGE OF CHANGE

Chapter One

*L*IKE IT OR NOT, THE WINDS BLOW

The day's first rays of sun reflected on the water as my older son, Chase, and I walked along the beach looking for shells. Ever since our first vacation on Florida's Sanibel Island when Chase was a toddler, he had loved this ritual of getting up at dawn to find the shells left by the tide. This was our time, a special adventure that neither Dad nor little brother was invited to share.

Heads down, we would shuffle along through the shallow water of the Gulf of Mexico, picking up shells and comparing our "finds." We would poke at strange sea life washed ashore, run after birds, and talk. As the rising sun broke through the mist, we would stop and watch it for a while, absorbing its warmth and marveling at its size. Then we would go back to our hotel and have breakfast.

It had been the same, year after year, but Chase was eleven now and enjoyed sleeping in. I feared he had outgrown our tradition. But at bedtime the first night, he reminded me, "Don't forget to set the alarm, Mom. We've got to get up early to find the good shells." And so I gladly checked the tide schedule and set my alarm so as not to miss the special time with Chase.

As we strolled along the beach, Chase reached out and took my hand. I was surprised to feel his long fingers entwined in mine; how little he resembled the pudgy toddler of years gone by. And I was even more surprised that this cool preteen was willing to hold on to me. At home he had long ago stopped holding my hand. But here, in the context of a comfortable, long-standing ritual and in a place of happy memories, he reached out and held my hand.

The significance of the moment overwhelmed me. He asked me a casual question, but I could hardly verbalize an answer. I cleared my throat, hoping he wouldn't hear the catch in my voice. I tried to sound befittingly casual; I tried not to hold his hand too tightly.

But I knew our relationship was changing. He was no longer a little boy who needed his mommy to protect him from waves and the creatures he imagined lurking in the waters. More often than not, he was protecting me these days, offering to carry grocery bags, holding doors, and taking care of me in ways that I found endearing but bittersweet.

Today Chase held my hand. But would he next year? I wasn't sure. I had to let him—even encourage him—to break his ties to me. Soon he would be walking a beach with a girl, holding her hand, finding shells to present to her. If I had done my job well, he would never dwell on how much he missed his walks with me. They would simply be experiences woven into the fabric of who he had become.

But I would miss my child. I would miss the dependence and simple trust. The wet kisses and sandy hugs. The squeals of delight at the treasures found and the gasps at stepping in the cold morning waves.

"Let's go back, Mom," Chase said, interrupting my thoughts. He dropped my hand and sprinted ahead on the beach, finding a shell and throwing it far into the waves. I looked at his tall frame and knew that going back was impossible. I could accept the changes or celebrate them, but I could not deny that our relationship would be different.

CHANGE HAPPENS

To paraphrase a popular bumper sticker, "Change happens." Whether we like it or not, whether we welcome it or resist it, the winds of change blow. Like the wind, change comes our way even if we don't see it; but we see its effects. As Christina Rossetti playfully writes:

> *Who has seen the wind?*
> *Neither you nor I:*
> *But when the trees bow down their heads,*
> *The wind is passing by.*

Over the past ten years my life has been full of change. I've seen and felt its effects. Some changes have been gradual, like the growth of my sons. Some have been sudden. Some I would call tragedies. Others I have noted only because my eyes have been opened, and I am allowing myself to grow.

Whether we like it or not, whether we welcome it or resist it, the winds of change blow.

As a parent, I understand the need for change and growth as an inevitable part of maturing. I remember when I was slightly older than Chase, a teenager who looked more like a woman than I felt. Working in my father's office one summer, I reached out to take his hand as we crossed a street. He held it gently and then later said, "You probably shouldn't hold my hand in public now. When people look at us they see a man and a woman instead of a father with his little girl." I look back now and realize how hard it was for my father to draw a boundary that would change our relationship forever. But he was right. It was no longer appropriate for me to express my feelings for him in public. And by giving up some of the expressions of affection in our relationship, he signaled to me that I was a woman now, that men saw me differently, and I needed to be aware of my actions.

As Paul reminds us in his letter to the Corinthians: "When I was a child, I talked like a child, I thought like a child, I reasoned like a child. When I became a man, I put childish ways behind me" (1 Cor. 13:11).

From the examples set by my parents, I've learned that trying to hold on to the past will only harm my child and our relationship. I have to let go of the old ways and await the potentially rocky days of adolescent independence and teenage rejection.

Change is both a promise and a threat.

As a mother I've learned that I must change and grow along with my children if I am to give them what they need at each new stage. It is part of what I am called to do as a parent.

But it isn't easy.

Change is both a promise and a threat. It represents everything we can hope for and all that we fear. Change comes out of the blue and turns our world upside down, or it offers the chance to reorder and renew. Change is the word most dreaded and most prayed for by every cancer patient; it can represent remission or recurrence.

CHANGE AS PROMISE

On one hand, we all want change. We want life to get better—in a controlled manner. I want my son to grow up and make a life of his own. I want him to mature, to become independent, to be a parent one day himself.

We hope for better days—and we work to make the changes that we think will usher them in. Every New Year's Day we make resolutions of change. What's more, every January, television, radio, and magazine commercials find new, improved ways to tell us that change is easy, even if we have never been able to pull it off before. Drink a diet milkshake, eat specially prepared foods, attend a group session, and *voila!* you can be thin, fit, lean, and mean by Easter.

Most of us know that change—even change for the better —is never that easy.

The gospel of change is preached by advertisers everywhere who know that the sale of their product depends on their ability to make consumers believe that change is not only possible, but it's also painless, harmless, and can happen while they sleep (for only $19.95—or your money back). And advertisers succeed. Why else would reasonable people plunk down money for thigh creams, wrinkle reducers, and hair-growth tonics? We believe that somewhere, somehow, someone will come up with a product that will make us more attractive, more productive, and incredibly popular—with no pain and always at a pleasing pace.

But no matter how much we want to believe in miracle products, most of us know that change—even change for the better—is never that easy. We jump on a new diet wagon only to fall off again in weeks or months. We watch as a friend vows to leave an abusive relationship but keeps finding an excuse to put it off. Despite claims to the contrary, the "promising" type of change is often painful.

CHANGE AS THREAT

And then there's change that comes as a threat—without our involvement or consent. Accidents happen. Companies downsize.

Spouses leave. Often without a warning, life as we know it comes to an abrupt, screeching stop, and we are left looking at broken pieces of what was once an orderly life.

I know what it's like to view changes as threats. My prayers used to be ones of thanks for what I had and protection so that nothing would change. At the office I had a sign on my desk that proclaimed to my staff "I hate surprises" just to remind them that I didn't want to be the last to know about a problem. I now know that what I really meant was that I didn't want any problems. I wanted my life to be calm and predictable. Change has never been easy for me. I like the security of knowing where the boundaries are and what is expected of me.

I remember the day that I was named editor of *Today's Christian Woman* magazine. I was twenty-five, full of optimism—and behind the facade, scared to death. I had never edited a national magazine before. What if I failed horribly and publicly?

I read every book on magazines, called every editor I knew, worked night and day on the first issue. With the help of a terrific staff, we put out that issue on time and with relatively few catastrophes. And then we put out the next issue and the next. Each was easier and more comfortable because I knew what to expect. What started as an exciting opportunity became routine.

Then one day I got another phone call. The magazine had been sold to a new company and would move to a new location. My "baby" was being handed over to new owners! Although I knew it was a business decision, and I could have continued in the job if I had wanted to move, I still couldn't get over the sense of loss. I loved everything about the magazine—the crazy deadlines and endless editing. The staff and the advertisers. The typefaces carefully chosen and the hundreds of photos reviewed to find the "perfect" one. The magazine was a big part of my life. And I was being told that I had to stop clinging to it and let it go on without me.

Although I am not a depressive person by nature, I went through a period of depression. I blew up over little things. I felt useless and frustrated. The change was almost more than I could handle.

CHANGE AS OPPORTUNITY AND CRISIS

At one point in my life I might have regarded the two kinds of change as opposites. I saw the promising change that we pursue as evidence of the control we want over our lives. I became a magazine editor with a great deal of "chutzpah" and the resolve to work night and day if I had to in order to succeed.

Crisis is an opportunity riding the dangerous wind.

Threatening change, however, showed me my lack of control. No matter how much I wanted to continue as editor, no matter how much I planned and tried to work it out, I was no longer part of the decisions being made. I was kindly thanked for the work I had done, but I was no longer needed.

Now I see that the two sides of change are more similar than different: Whether changes interrupt our lives seemingly by choice or seemingly by chance, they are divine opportunities.

In fact, the Chinese symbols for *crisis* are identical to those for the word *opportunity*. Literally translated the symbols read, "Crisis is an opportunity riding the dangerous wind."

I learned more about this a few years ago, when I signed up for three days of sailing lessons and learned the lesson of turning toward the wind. . . .

QUESTIONS FOR REFLECTION

1. Think of your own childhood. When did you recognize points of change and maturing at the time? Looking back now, what do you see? Do you see times that were difficult then but are understandable now in light of your mature understanding?

2. How did your parents encourage you to change? How did they hold on to you in ways that were less than healthy? If you are a parent, what are you doing differently with your own children?

3. In what ways is change hard for you today? Is it difficult to see your body aging? Do changes in relationships hurt you? Do you often wish that things could be as they used to be?

Chapter Two

𝒯URN TOWARD THE WIND

T he cool, gentle breeze blew across my face, providing comfort from the heat of the sun. As our sailboat cut through the waves, the sound of the water lapping against the hull was almost melodic. I dragged my hand in the water, closed my eyes, and leaned back to enjoy the ride. We were heading toward the Bay Bridge, out of the calm waters of Annapolis harbor and into the expanse of the Chesapeake Bay.

I waved to another boat that passed several yards from our bow. Lettering on our mainsail declared that we were a boat from one of the local sailing schools. Experienced sailors gave us plenty of room, knowing that we were "student drivers" who didn't always know the rules or how to respond to new conditions. I laughed as the captain of the other boat steered away from our course.

My peaceful reverie ended when I felt the wind shift. The once taut sail began to ripple, slowing us down and making a dissonant sound. "Prepare to come about!" yelled the instructor.

My body tensed. I knew what her instruction meant: I leaned forward and yanked the jib line from its clamp, pulling back with all my strength so the end of the line wouldn't fly free. My job was to mind the front sail—the jib—and keep it in sync with the mainsail. Most of the time it was a simple job of "trimming" the sail, or making the surface more taut so that it worked more efficiently. But when it was time to "come about," I had real work to do.

I coaxed the sail from one side of the boat to the other, working with the rest of the crew to do it at the same time the rudder turned and the mainsail swung about. Having done this before, I knew to stoop down to allow the boom to fly over my head. As our center of gravity shifted, I moved my weight to the balls of my feet to steady myself.

"Ready about!" I called back in reply.

"Helms a lee!" yelled our instructor, telling me the boat was turning leeward. Suddenly the once calm sailboat became a cacophony of sounds and movements—the lines cranked through their housings, the sail fluttered, the boom clanked, and everyone on board shifted position.

I used every muscle to pull in the jib line on the opposite side. At first the sail resisted, and then it flew across the mast and filled with air. I pulled back an inch at a time, making the sail taut as the person holding the rudder told us we were on course. And then we took off in a direction almost opposite of where we'd been.

"Good job!" yelled our instructor as our crew members patted each other on the back and congratulated ourselves on remembering what we had learned in the classroom. I secured the jib line and relaxed again, my heart resuming a slower rhythm as my muscles unknotted and my breathing calmed.

FACING CHANGE

Before learning to sail, I had watched boats gliding effortlessly across the water of the Bay and imagined them to be floating islands of peace. But once I'd had a few sailing lessons, I knew that there was nothing more stressful—or more relaxing—than sailing.

I had always assumed that the art of sailing was nothing more than positioning a boat so that the prevailing breeze filled the sails and pushed the boat along. If the wind blew from west to east, I believed the boat would sail from west to east. How surprised I was to discover that sailors are often sailing toward the wind.

As my husband and I sat in sailing class with a group of young and old from all walks of life, we struggled to understand the principles that would guide us when we actually began to sail our own boats. It didn't matter who we were; the winds would treat us the same. On a boat sailors are judged by their ability to respond to the wind, not by status or position.

TURN TOWARD THE WIND

Face the winds of change and use them to propel you forward.

Since my husband had studied engineering principles to prepare him for a career in architecture, he patiently tried to explain aerodynamics to me without much luck. I don't know if I will ever understand why the wind blowing over sails creates a vacuum that propels the boat forward. But sitting in one of my first sailing classes, trying to learn about jibbing and beating, I was struck by a spiritual lesson so meaningful that I think of it whenever I see—no less step onto—a sailboat.

Our teacher was showing us how to find the wind and then aim our boats at an angle toward it. She stood at the blackboard, drawing diagrams and excitedly explaining what we would soon experience: "It is a great thrill to find that perfect spot, have your sails ready, and feel your boat take off," she said.

For a second my attention wandered from the instructor and her diagrams. Another voice spoke to my spirit. It was as if God were whispering, *See, that's what I want you to do with your life. I want you to face the winds of change and use them to propel you forward.*

This struck me as more than a philosophical thought. It was a lifeline that God threw to me at a critical time. Three years ago I had lost a baby, now my father was dying of a brain tumor, and a dear friend had just succumbed to breast cancer. I was feeling disoriented, undone, and unsteadied by the shifting winds of change that had battered me.

What next? I had begun to cry out in my prayers. Usually positive and optimistic, I was beginning to understand how Job must have felt when struck with one blow after another. I had resisted the pushes and pulls on my life for as long as I could. I'd come to a point where I wanted to simply give up and let them toss me to and fro.

But there I sat, not in church but in a sailing class with a room full of would-be sailors from all walks of life, hearing God's voice. *Turn toward the wind,* he seemed to say. *Let it propel you in new directions.*

My instructor's voice broke into my consciousness. "Although you can't sail directly into the wind, you can come very close. Early sailors didn't realize this and were forced to head in the direction of the wind."

As I listened I realized I was ready for a new direction in life. "What are you trying to teach me, God?" I asked over and over in the next weeks and months.

Don't resist the wind. Turn toward it, and you will find me, he seemed to say.

THE WIND AND THE SPIRIT

I didn't understand the meaning at the time. I'm sure I don't fully understand it even now. But the call to face the winds of change resonated deep inside me on a level that defied human logic and inhibitions and spoke directly to my soul. Now, as I try to explain this journey, it seems that I am trying to define the indefinable—map a course that is still a mystery, as mysterious as the wind itself.

*If you have chosen to live a life of the Spirit,
the winds will still blow.*

I learned later that in Hebrew, Greek, and Latin, the word for *wind* and for *Spirit* are the same: *ruach* in Hebrew; *pneuma* in Greek; *spiritus* in Latin. Jesus himself gave a spiritual lesson based on the mysterious quality of the wind and made a correlation between the wind and the movement of the Holy Spirit in our lives. In John 3:8 Jesus says to Nicodemus, "The wind blows wherever it pleases. You hear its sound, but you cannot tell where it comes from or where it is going. So it is with everyone born of the Spirit."

If you have chosen to live a life of the Spirit, the winds will still blow. You will not be exempt because of status or power. You cannot beg God to spare you because you are not strong enough. The winds will help make you strong. They will blow and you will have to respond. If you choose to turn away, you will miss the chance to grow. As Paul Tournier observes in *Creative Suffering:* "The problem of deprivation is not to be solved by shutting one's eyes, but by facing it courageously."

I invite you to join me on a journey of discovering the lessons the Spirit has in store for those who turn toward the winds of change. In the introduction I mentioned my friend Jack. Let me give you a few more details of the gale winds that blew through his life several years before they blew through mine.

QUESTIONS FOR REFLECTION

1. What are the most difficult winds of change you have faced? How have you responded to them?
2. What can you learn from those close to you who have dealt with change? How have people resisted changes? How have you seen people respond positively?
3. In what ways have you seen the spirit of God in the winds of change in your life?

Chapter Three

*W*HEN BAD THINGS HAPPEN

Jack pulled into his driveway and turned off the car. With a weary sigh, he dragged his heavy briefcase from the passenger seat, got out, and walked up his sidewalk. It had been a long day, and in his briefcase he carried another hour or two of work. He would get to it after the kids went to bed and would probably still be working when Shelly said good night. That had been the pattern for the last couple of years. Some days he didn't know how much longer he could keep it up.

As he inserted his key into the lock, Jack paused for a moment to admire the polished oak door. *It is a beautiful house,* he thought with pride. He knew that Shelly loved having such an impressive house. He knew that most of the people living in such a prestigious neighborhood had worked a lifetime to afford their houses. Jack wasn't even thirty; his whole life was ahead of him.

"I'm home," he called out as he walked in and set his briefcase in the hallway. He waited for a moment, listening for the typical sounds of the kids playing in the bathtub or chasing each other in pre-bedtime games. "Shelly?" he called. "What's for dinner?" He sniffed the air, usually able to discern what the family had eaten an hour or two before. Walking into the kitchen, he looked for the plate that usually awaited him. Shelly had long ago given up on having a family dinner. Now she set a place for him; on the rare occasion when he made it home on time, he joined the family. Otherwise, she simply covered his plate and left it on the counter.

"Shelly?" he called. And then he saw the note placed under a mug where his full plate usually sat. He picked it up and stared at it for a long time, thinking his eyes must be playing tricks, wondering if it were a cruel hoax.

"I can't take it anymore," the note said in Shelly's girlish handwriting. "The kids are at your parents' house. I need some time alone. I can't go on like this."

Jack slumped to the kitchen floor and read the note over again. *Haven't I given her everything she wanted?* he asked himself. The house, the new furniture, the nice vacations . . .

That morning everything had been fine—or so he thought. Perhaps the kids had been a little more boisterous than usual. He tried to remember his conversation with Shelly. They'd talked about dry cleaning and getting a baby-sitter for Saturday so they could go to the company barbecue. Shelly hadn't seemed upset. In fact, hadn't things been going better after the bumpy times they'd had in the past? *She's just having a bad day,* Jack told himself. *I'll pick up the kids, give her a break, and everything will be fine.*

But everything was not fine. Shelly returned in a few days and then left, taking the children with her. Jack begged her to go to counseling with him, but all she said was, "It's too late for that."

Eventually Jack heard the rumors. Shelly had a boyfriend, someone she'd been seeing for months. While he'd been traveling and working late, she'd hired baby-sitters and gone out. He'd never even suspected.

"Who is he?" he asked her angrily one day as they spoke on the phone.

"Why, don't you know?" she asked. "It's Mike. We love each other and plan to get married."

Mike was a close friend of Jack's. They'd gone jogging together, watched baseball games, helped each other on household projects. The betrayal was almost too great to bear. *Shelly and Mike.* Jack was angry, humiliated, and hurt. He had never even suspected. He thought back over conversations he'd had with Mike. He couldn't find a clue that something had been amiss.

For the first time, Jack broke down and wept. He sobbed as he cried out to God, "Why?" He had always wanted a nice, secure home. He was a good provider, and he tried to be a loving father. He took his family to church every Sunday. Sure, he could be tough in business. And Shelly had complained that he wasn't sensitive enough to her, but he was basically a good and honest guy who tried to do the right thing. How could God let this happen to him?

SECURITY FENCES

Jack believed what many of us hold on to as long as we can: As long as we try to live the right way, chances are everything will be fine. To believe differently is to let ourselves be vulnerable, and humanly, that is the last way we want to live. Day after day we lock our doors, take our vitamins, and believe that if we live by the rules, we will be all right. Sure, we know that lightning sometimes strikes. We read about random violence and airline crashes. In response, we do the "reasonable" things: We buy security alarms; we ask our travel agents to book us on safe airlines preferably in a seat over the wing; we warn our children to stay away from trees in bad weather. It doesn't matter how much we believe in God, our human response to the threat of tragedy is to protect ourselves and our families.

Underlying that desire to protect ourselves is a suspicion that harm is always caused by human error. Modern Americans seem obsessed with the notion that tragedy can be avoided. As one commentator wrote, "the idea that our individual lives and the nation's life can and should be risk-free has grown to be an obsession, driven far and deep into American attitudes."[1]

We are convinced that bad things happen because people are stupid, take risks, or in some way deserve what befalls them. We want desperately to believe that tragedy can be explained.

Day after day we lock our doors, take our vitamins, and believe that if we live by the rules, we will be all right.

⤳ ⤶

One of the most frustrating airline tragedies occurred one Sunday morning in 1992 when United flight 737 crashed into the ground instead of landing safely in Colorado Springs. Several air force pilots witnessed the tragedy. Months of investigations confirmed what the eyewitnesses said at the time: There didn't seem to be any reason for it. Years later it remains as one of the two U.S. airplane crashes never explained away by pilot error, weather conditions, or equipment failure. Everyone was playing by the rules, but the crash was still fatal.

In Jack's mind, he had played by the rules, too. But Shelly hadn't. She had broken the trust of the marriage and betrayed him with his close friend. Once he got over the initial shock, he was angry. *How could she do this to him and the kids?* he wondered. *How could she be so selfish?*

FENCING US IN

When I think of Jack's story I am reminded of my own reaction to the news of his marriage breaking up. Tom and I had been married almost as long as Jack and Shelly, although we hadn't started our family. I was shocked by Shelly's behavior. After all, she was the mother of four young children. By all appearances, Jack had set her up with a lifestyle that was the envy of everyone around. Shouldn't she have been grateful?

At first I judged Shelly, and then I turned to Jack and looked for ways to blame him. Shelly may have been ungrateful, but Jack was surely an insensitive materialist, intent only on proving himself at work and in the acquisition game. Working with him was no picnic. He often cut people off in meetings, implying that they didn't know what they were talking about. He made unilateral decisions that affected everyone without any concern about the impact. He always seemed to be in a hurry, certainly not someone you could go to with a problem.

Yes, in my mind it made sense that Jack's marriage broke up. I could point my finger and name someone to blame. Why did I have to "make sense" of it? I had my own security fences to keep intact. If Jack's marriage could break up, anyone's could. That was a thought too threatening to contemplate. I tried to ignore that I had always thought Jack and Shelly were a wonderful couple, that I had seen evidence that they loved each other and adored their children.

To protect my own world, I put Jack's divorce in an "I'm so sorry" category and went back to my own predictable life—my security fence unmoved. I felt immune from tragedy.

At the time I thought about sending Jack a note, but I never got around to it. He didn't seem like the kind of guy who would appreciate sympathy anyway.

If I could just try hard enough,
surely everything would be all right.

Soon after that I heard that Jack had lost his job. Then I lost track of him for a while. My own career was going along just fine. I was busy starting my own magazine publishing company, and everything was going well. I was just too busy to slow down and deal with someone else's pain. I was working harder than ever. Tom and I were making plans to have a family. By the time my first son was born, I had everything worked out. With a business of my own, I was able to accommodate motherhood by bringing my baby and a baby-sitter to the office. I could even nurse my baby during the day.

Sure, I had my frustrations. My love of control ran headfirst into the erratic schedule of a newborn. I struggled to succeed at motherhood as if it were a career and found few benchmarks to measure my progress. My husband helped as much as he could, but I felt like I was responsible for making everything work well. If I could just try hard enough, surely everything would be all right.

FAIRY-TALE ENDINGS

We carefully planned for another child and, like clockwork, I became pregnant again. I was living happily ever after. But then my doctor noticed that I was gaining weight rapidly. And by my second checkup, he knew why: We were expecting twins.

Wait a minute. This is not in my plans. How can I run a business and deal with two more babies? How can I care for three children at once? The questions overwhelmed me, and yet I knew that somehow we would cope. We bought a station wagon, bought two of everything, and waited.

I read all of the books and felt secure that I had a great doctor. I did everything right: I took my vitamins, had weekly checkups, and even did moderate exercises until I grew too big to move much at all. Because I was thirty-four, I was considered a risk for early labor, so I took to bed for six critical weeks during my second trimester. I lay on a couch and worked from home by phone and fax, having meetings in my living room as my stomach grew larger each day. Every time I went in for a checkup my doctor assured me that I was having a model pregnancy.

CONFRONTING REALITY

On a beautiful August day I went in for yet another routine checkup. I was in my third trimester—seven months along—considered the home stretch for twin pregnancies. Few go fully to term. Carrying two babies is more than most bodies can take for nine months.

As I waddled into the obstetrician's office I greeted each of the nurses by name. I had seen them so often that we had become friends. They were interested in my progress and helpful with my questions.

"Have you decided on any names yet?" one nurse asked as I signed in. Knowing that I was expecting a girl and a boy, the nurses had been helping me come up with names. "How about Taylor and Tyler?"

"I'd never be able to keep the two straight!" I responded.

At this point in my pregnancy the doctor had ordered an ultrasound every week in order to chart the progress of the babies. With so little room for them to grow, he wanted to be sure they had adequate space to develop. My usual technician was on vacation, so a new woman ushered me into the ultrasound room.

As I searched my memory for the Bible verses I knew well, only one seemed to fit: "My God, my God, why have you forsaken me?"

I knew the routine well by now. Lying on a table in the darkened room, I pulled up my top to reveal my huge stomach. The technician turned on the screen, rubbed my belly with gel, and passed the monitor over my skin, revealing the images within me.

There was my little boy, active as ever. His hands were moving near his face as if he were waving to us. We laughed. Then the technician eased the monitor over his chest and watched for a few moments as his little heart beat rhythmically. "Everything looks perfect!" she announced.

Next she moved to the other side of my belly, revealing the outline of my baby girl. "Wake up," I said, nudging her. The probe passed over her several times, but she continued to sleep. And then I realized that the monitor was showing her heart and it, too, was motionless. The technician dropped the monitor in a panic. "I've got to get the doctor," she said as she ran from the room.

I lay there in the darkened room with my stomach exposed and tried to pray. "Let this be a mistake," I begged. As the minutes passed I began to feel more and more afraid. And I felt something else. I felt abandoned. As I searched my memory for the Bible verses I knew well, only one seemed to fit: "My God, my God, why have you for-saken me?"

The doctor finally appeared, squeezed my hand and picked up the monitor. "Over here," I pointed out, helping to find the area where my little girl's heart should be beating. His experienced hand held the probe over the little chest. The outline of the heart was visible on the screen, but still there was no movement. Gently he wiped the gel off of my stomach, pulled down my top, and helped me sit up. "I'm sorry," he said as he hugged me.

It sounded strangely like "It is finished."

In shock, I followed him to his office, where I struggled to stay in control. "What happened to her? Will the same thing happen to my baby boy? Should we go to the hospital now and deliver him?"

I asked question after question as my doctor sat quietly. Finally he said, "I wish I had answers. But I am only a doctor. Now God is in control."

His words shocked me. I had never heard him speak of God before. I wanted him to give me medical advice; instead he spoke of God. I wanted him to assure me that I was still part of the process; instead he reminded me that there were no answers.

"Go home and get some rest. I'll call a specialist at the hospital and schedule you for more tests tomorrow," he said.

I wanted him to assure me that I was still part of the process; instead he reminded me that there were no answers.

I called my husband, but he was in a meeting, and I didn't want to disturb him. Instead I got back into my car and drove home, stop-ping on the way for groceries. There was so little I could control. Somehow, buying groceries made me feel better.

Over the next days I saw specialist after specialist. An amnio-centesis revealed that my baby boy's lungs were immature. To deliver him early would risk his health. No test determined the cause of my baby girl's death.

I was left to try to carry my babies—one dead, the other alive—for as long as I could. The anxiety was almost unbearable. Every time I fell asleep I awoke again to nudge my baby boy and feel his movement. Meanwhile my baby girl's body began to produce toxins that would eventually harm me and my other baby. Daily blood tests showed the level in my system; every few days they inserted a long needle into my stomach to determine the development of my baby boy's lungs.

> *I grieved that life as I had known it was over.*
> *Bad things happened to me, too.*
>
> ~€ ᦇ~

After three weeks of this nightmare I finally went into labor. They delivered my babies during an emergency C-section, taking one to the morgue and the other to neonatal intensive care. I lay in the recovery room not knowing whether I would see my baby boy alive. It was a Catholic hospital and a nun came by to pray with me. I listened to her words, but I still felt alone. *Why is God punishing me?* I wondered.

Hours later they brought me my baby boy. He was tiny but breathing on his own. As I held him, the tears of the last three weeks finally flowed. I held him tightly and grieved for his twin sister. And I grieved that life as I had known it was over. Bad things happened to me, too. God and I no longer had a bargain. I was not exempt from tragedy, either.

It didn't seem fair then, and it still doesn't make sense to me now, even as I look across the dinner table at my six-year-old son and wonder what it would be like if a six-year-old daughter were sitting at his side. The pain is still real, the questions still unanswered.

IS "WHY?" THE RIGHT QUESTION?

And yet one thing I know for sure: Bad things happen even when we follow the rules. Tragedies don't befall people just because they are stupid or careless or insensitive. I had been fortunate—and naive—before I experienced my own first loss. There have been others since, and, I suspect, there will be more to come. Sitting on an ash heap, Job said, "Man is born to trouble as surely as sparks fly upward" (Job 5:7)—or as surely as the wind blows.

> *Bad things happen even when we follow the rules.*
>
> ~€ ᦇ~

Why do bad things happen? Depending on your theology, you could argue for days about the nature of pain and evil. Entire books have been written to answer the question, including *Why Us? When Bad Things Happen to God's People* by Warren Wiersbe and the now classic *Where Is God When It Hurts* by Philip Yancey.

It's a question as old as the book of Job, which some say is the oldest biblical writing. Warren Wiersbe notes that the book of Job includes more than three hundred questions, many asked by Job himself. But Job's why questions were silenced in the presence of almighty God. Suddenly Job began asking a new kind of question: "I am unworthy—how can I reply to you?" (Job 40:4). Christopher Morley writes: "I had a million questions to ask God: but when I met Him, they all fled my mind; it didn't seem to matter."[2]

And in this regard Wiersbe says simply, "When you and I hurt deeply, what we really need is not an explanation from God but a revelation of God."[3]

God wants us, his children, to grow to the point that we are able to stop asking, "Why?" and start asking, "What am I to learn?"

Yancey sees this clearly in Jesus' teaching in the Gospels:

> The disciples wanted to look backward, to find out "Why?" Jesus redirected their attention. Consistently, he points forward, answering a different question: "To what end?" And that, I believe, offers a neat summary of the Bible's approach to the problem of pain. To backward-looking questions of cause, to the "Why?" questions, it gives no definitive answer. But it does hold out hope for the future, that even suffering can be transformed or "redeemed."[4]

Yancey calls pain "the megaphone of God." God wants our attention. As I see it, God does not want us to suffer any more than I want my sons to skin their knees or get bad grades or have fights with their friends. But during those moments when my children cry in pain or frustration, I hold them and try to teach them a lesson that they are now open to learn because they can see their need.

❧　❧

After losing our daughter, my first questions were "Why? Why me? Why us?" My fences had been ripped down by a gale-force wind and I was railing at God—like Job.

I now see that God was patiently waiting for me to ask a new question. He was waiting for me to listen for his answer.

It would still take awhile for me to get to the point where I could turn toward the wind, not fight against it. It would be awhile before I could see that gale-force winds are not simply a destructive force that upsets us; if we are willing to receive them, they can be an instructive force that teaches us. It would take me awhile before I could turn and face those very things I once feared most—pain, death, loss, and humiliation—and not ask "Why?" but "What am I to learn that will help me to grow? What am I to learn that will enable me to help others grow?"

God wants us to grow to the point that we are able to stop asking, "Why?" and start asking, "What am I to learn?"

Let me return to Jack's story to show how God started to show me that there is a better way of handling crisis.

At the time of our loss, we received cards from many caring people who tried to soothe our pain. I remember opening a card from Jack. His note was short, but he seemed to know something about my pain. It was clear that he knew about suffering; he, too, had felt loss. He had a new job now—not as prestigious as the one in the past—and he only saw his children on weekends. He had not lived happily ever after and neither had I.

I was struck that some people tried to cheer me up or encouraged me to put the pain behind me. Some tried to emphasize the positive: "At least you have one baby" or look for answers: "There was probably something wrong with the baby anyway." But those who comforted me the most were notes like the one from Jack, words from people who felt the pain with me and did not encourage me to turn away. I felt as if my experience had ushered me into a new fraternity. I was suddenly joined to others who knew what it meant to have the winds of change tear you from your safe moorings.

I didn't understand it then, but I see now that I was beginning a journey that Jack was already on. It is a road populated by those who have experienced—and faced—pain; a journey through the desert in search of The Way.

QUESTIONS FOR REFLECTION

1. How have you responded to the tragedies that have befallen others? Do you try to fix their problems? Do you know how to simply care for others during a crisis?

2. Think of some of the most difficult times in your life. Who has helped you the most? What has that person done or said that comforted you?

3. Do you know a modern-day Job—someone who has suffered a great deal? How has that person responded? What can you learn from his or her example?

4. Reread the book of Job. What does the book reveal about why suffering comes into our life?

5. What have you learned from the difficult times you have endured? Did God seem far away as you suffered? As you look back, do you see his hand in your recovery?

Chapter Four

WHEN WE INITIATE CHANGE

Sometimes change rips through life like a hurricane, uprooting all we hold dear. Other times it blows like a gentle breeze, awakening us to the promise of something different, something more. The second kind of change beckons us gently. If we are unwilling to feel its stirrings, it passes on, leaving us with only a memory of what might have been.

And yet questions can still haunt us even when we seek out the promise of change. Perhaps it's because we ultimately are not in control of the direction the wind takes, even when we are open to following it.

JOAN'S STORY

My friend Joan first felt the breeze of change when her children left home. With two boys just two years apart in age, she had enjoyed a full life as a mother. "I was used to coaching, organizing bake sales, timing swim races. . . . When my boys went off to college, my life seemed so empty. I felt depressed and purposeless."

Major changes in Joan's life came as a result of the passing of time—the slow changes that come as children grow up and away. But those changes caused a discontent that made Joan look for ways to give further meaning to her life. As a breeze blew in her life, she saw potential. She asked if it was meant to be an opportunity for her.

Joan thought about going back to school to update her teaching credentials but was discouraged by the number of courses she would have to take. Then she saw an ad in her community paper seeking someone to be a part-time editorial assistant. On a whim, she applied for the job. She was shocked when she went to the interview and was hired on the spot.

"I panicked," she says. "I didn't think of myself as a working woman. I didn't have the right clothes. I didn't even know if I'd like going to the same place every day. What if I didn't get along with the other staff members? I nearly called them and told them I couldn't take the job."

But Joan did take the job and after two weeks was happier than she had been in years. She was praised for her organizational skills, and the younger women in the office began to affectionately call her "Mom," because she often gave them advice or acted protectively toward them. When a full-time job as assistant editor opened up, the editor told Joan that she was the leading candidate. When she came home to tell her husband, Harry, about the job, she was surprised by his reaction.

"Harry had been happy when I took the first job. It was part-time and not very impressive. But the idea that I might take on a real, professional position seemed to offend Harry. He had always been the breadwinner in the family. He had a good job as a salesman, but he was probably never going to be a manager. I didn't know what to do," Joan confessed.

Encouraged by the other staff members, Joan accepted the position. Her new job meant that she wasn't home in time to have dinner on the table by 6:00. It meant that vacation time had to be scheduled not just around Harry's job but around Joan's as well. And over the months Harry clearly became very unhappy.

"I considered quitting, but that seemed so silly," said Joan. "And besides, I was angry that Harry couldn't let me have my chance to accomplish something. My paycheck meant that the boys didn't have to take out school loans, and that seemed to help the entire family. Harry just couldn't deal with the fact that I had a professional position that I enjoyed and did well at."

Joan suggested counseling, but Harry refused. "I don't need a counselor; I just need a wife," he said. At that point Joan worked out a different schedule so she could start her day earlier and end in time to be home for an early dinner. Harry was unimpressed. Joan found herself downplaying her job when Harry was around and trying to build Harry up in front of their friends. But no matter what she did, Harry was petulant.

"Even the kids could see that I was happy and fulfilled and that Harry wouldn't give me a chance," Joan said.

But during one school vacation her younger son confronted her: "Why can't things just be the way they were?" he asked. "Why did you have to get a job?"

Joan spent hours replaying the chain of events. Changes in her life had affected her family and her relationships. How had this happened? How had the winds of change led her into churning waters?

All she had wanted to do was stay busy. She had been depressed without the boys; her depression had been an emotional drain on Harry. That seemed so long ago. Now everything had turned around; her own happiness seemed to be causing more problems than she'd started out with. She hadn't sought the job promotion. But she was good at what she did, and she couldn't imagine pretending that she wasn't. And yet—she loved Harry and her children and didn't think a job was worth ruining her marriage.

> *Her own happiness seemed to be causing more problems than she'd started out with.*

In time Joan sought out the help of a counselor who gently explained what was happening. Joan had grown considerably; Harry was stuck in a comfortable place and didn't want to move. Joan wasn't causing Harry's misery; he was. But Joan's actions had initiated the frustration in their marriage, and the counselor openly suggested that Joan and Harry's relationship might not survive the strain.

Joan cried and prayed, worried, and doubted herself. Finally she confronted Harry. "Harry, I love you and want us to have a good relationship," she said. "But I also want to do something productive with my life and not have to apologize for it. I'm going to keep my job, and I hope you will support me. But if you don't, I'm not going to make excuses because things aren't the way they used to be. You'll just have to get used to living with a working woman."

Harry's reaction was worse than Joan had feared. Instead of getting angry, he simply walked out of the house without a word. When he finally returned at midnight, Joan had been crying for hours. "Okay, I'll learn to deal with it," Harry said without much conviction. "I guess I've been stubborn and proud. I'd rather live with a working woman like you than with anyone else."

To say that Joan and Harry have lived happily ever after would be an exaggeration. They have struggled and worked at a marriage that was once comfortable and untroubled. But they are both at the point where they can say that the relationship is stronger today than it was before Joan went to work. And Harry has grown to the point where he is proud of Joan's accomplishments. He even occasionally cooks dinner for the two of them.

LEAVING THE SAFETY ZONE

Although we sometimes think we can control what we initiate, we often find that one simple decision begins a series of events that may or may not be what we intended to accomplish. We may wish we had never left the safe and solid shore.

When change comes into our life unexpectedly, we tend to react with shock or denial. But when we make the effort to seek out change, we ride an emotional roller coaster that runs from the highs of excitement to the depths of self-doubt. Enthusiasm can turn to panic. And worse, we blame ourselves for any problems that arise from our self-imposed change. *Why couldn't I have left well enough alone?*

Change can prompt growth. Growth includes pain. Sometimes we cannot stand the pain and so we resist the changes that have begun. We remember fondly the way things were and forget what caused us to initiate change. Even the pain of the past and the dysfunction of our situations can seem minor compared to what we have gotten ourselves into.

When we make the effort to seek out change,
we ride an emotional roller coaster that runs from the highs
of excitement to the depths of self-doubt.

Years ago when Cynthia Swindoll confronted her husband, Chuck, she wasn't sure how he'd react. She was frustrated with her situation: taking care of four young children and being in a totally supportive role while Chuck was out doing the "exciting" work of being a minister in a growing church and enjoying an increasing national presence as an author.

Chuck was a macho guy from Texas, but Cynthia knew that he had an open heart and a desire to listen to God. So Cynthia prayed— and then she confronted.

"I'll never forget that day," said Chuck, as I interviewed him for a story on change in the magazine *Today's Better Life* (now *Aspire*). "I knew that if I gave Cynthia the chance to grow, I would have to do things differently. I had it pretty good up until that point."

Chuck did listen to Cynthia's concerns, and together they began to make changes. He gave her more opportunities to use her organizational and leadership skills in the fledgling organization Insight for Living which developed Chuck's radio ministry. He took more responsibility for the family. It wasn't always easy or pleasant. But today Chuck and Cynthia have a marriage that both say is better than they ever imagined it would be.

Chuck, now president of Dallas Theological Seminary and a well-known writer and speaker, says, "Cynthia can do things I could never do. She has talents I don't have. In running Insight for Living, she allows me to be a preacher, not an administrator. Without her we wouldn't have the ministry we have."

Was the journey easy? Both Chuck and Cynthia say no. Was it worth it? *Absolutely,* they say in unison.

Cynthia didn't know how initiating change would affect her marriage. Chuck could have reacted differently, and they might have spent years in a frustrating situation. Seeking change brings no guarantees of outcome.

THE JOURNEY BEGINS

Whether change finds us or we seek it, whether we are confronted by our failings or dissatisfied despite our successes, whether we are struck by a hurricane or summoned by a breeze, when we say yes to change, we say yes to God. It is as if we give back to the Creator the right to create. If we are walking with God, he can direct our paths. He can also help us discern when a breeze of change is divine or simply human yearning.

The Lord promises to show us the way. He does not say he will lay out the plan in twenty-four hours or less, nor does he promise to tell us what will come after the next step. Sometimes he wants us to learn patience, and so we wait. Other times he teaches obedience, and opportunities come faster than we can comprehend their significance. But throughout all of it, he asks us to keep our eyes on him.

The Lord promises to show us the way.

If we are fully focused on God, something we read may provide insight. A friend's words may give us a piece of the puzzle. A sermon might seem to be preached directly to us. But we should never seek God through friends or books or sermons. When we do so, we are really looking for information to factor into our own plan. We aren't ready to hear the words God wants us to hear directly from his Word. For the most part, what we get from friends is human logic. But when the Spirit of God moves, logic can seem foolish.

Once God has revealed his plan to us, our own road maps seem silly. It is as if we are planning a trip via the highway, and he is taking us on a supersonic jet. Even though we have carefully measured the advantages of taking Highway 10 over Highway 5, it makes little difference to the jet screaming above.

When the Spirit of God moves,
logic can seem foolish.

We are human and his ways are not ours. Even when we come to the point of knowing we need change, we find it is difficult to keep from trying to fix ourselves rather than letting God work on us. Actually, even if and when we realize that only God can truly change us, we find it humanly difficult to cooperate in the process. God needs our consent, our willingness to let him work. He won't barge into our lives to take over. He asks us to trust; he asks us to look and see what we have never seen before.

As we change, we begin to strip away the carefully constructed fences and walls that keep us from seeing the truth. And in that process we often discover answers to questions we might wish had gone unasked.

QUESTIONS FOR REFLECTION

1. Is there an area in your life where you feel discontent? Have you asked God to show you if he is trying to prepare you for a change?

2. Is it difficult for you to initiate change? How do you and your spouse react differently to change?

3. Is there an area in your marriage or in another close relationship that needs changing? Have you prayed about it? Is there a time when you can discuss it with the other person?

4. Have you ever initiated a change and then regretted it? Looking back, what can you learn from what happened?

5. Do you long for the "good old days"? Do you prefer the past to the present? Have you asked God to help you live today with the expectation that he will reveal himself to you?

Part Two

WHEN CHANGE HAPPENS IN US

Chapter Five

TWO HARD QUESTIONS

One day I sat at a restaurant tapping my foot and waiting for my friend Amy to show up. We had planned to meet at 12:30. It was already 1:00. In my mind I replayed the various times Amy had been late or had not shown up at all, and the general indifference she showed to my schedule. I was fuming by the time she showed up at 1:15. "Sorry. Got stuck in traffic," she said breezily as she sat down.

She'll never change, I thought to myself. And then I realized that as much as I believed that people do change, that I had changed, and that I was writing a book about change, I still had to acknowledge that some people really don't want to change.

Maybe they are afraid or unwilling to leave behind what they know. Maybe they don't want to go through the difficult times associated with growth. Or maybe they aren't willing to look hard at themselves and realize that their problems are greater than what they can handle on their own.

IN THE DUMPS

A few years ago I traveled to Guatemala with World Vision, the international relief and development organization, with a group of other women donors. We were starting a program called "Women of Vision" to link women in the U.S. directly to projects helping women and children overseas. One of the most heartbreaking scenes of that trip was at the end of a bus ride to the city dump just a few miles from our comfortable hotel in Guatemala City. I could smell the dump before I saw it. The horrible stench made us cover our noses and close the bus windows. It was hard to imagine anyone living in the neighborhoods near the pile of rotting, putrid garbage that baked each day in the hot sun.

As the bus approached the site, I saw smoke rising from brightly colored piles. And then I noticed that the entire mountain of garbage seemed to be moving. I was shocked to discover that the mounds of garbage were covered by grimy people—many of them children—searching for any piece of food or "treasure" they could find. Most of the people lived in the dump, creating little shelters out of the garbage itself. I saw one little girl emerge from a paper box, her face smudged with dirt, her hair tangled and filthy. She had a cut on one leg and the blood mixed with the filth clinging to her shin. At first I thought, *She needs to clean that wound.* And then I realized that the box was her house. She had probably never bathed in her young life, and the germs infesting her cut were ones she lived with night and day. I was suddenly confronted by the overwhelming problems of the "dump people."

As our bus approached, children ran up to it, begging at the windows for money or food. My first instinct was to jump off the bus and rescue these little ones from the dirt and disease. But our guides were very clear: We were to stay on the bus with the doors closed. To step out was to risk our lives. Most of these children were already very violent, they explained. Their lives were a constant battle for survival, and many had already learned that to live in the dump meant fighting, sometimes killing. To escape the reality of this awful existence, many inhaled glue or any other hallucinogen they could find. Sometimes they became crazed and very aggressive.

Back at our hotel at the end of the day, we asked what we could do to save these children. Could we adopt a child and take him or her to a better life? Patiently, the World Vision staff explained that if we took these children out of the dump, they would still be violent. If we brought them back to our nice hotel, bathed them, and gave them plenty of food, they would run back to the dump as quickly as they could. That is the life they know. They are comfortable in that filthy rut.

But World Vision does have a program that works to change these children inside and out: a brightly painted school on the edge of the dump. The dump children are curious about the school and sometimes come to see what the other children are doing. They see them laughing and learning to read. They see them neatly dressed and sitting politely. And sometimes one of the children from the dump grows curious enough that he asks if he, too, can come to school. That is when the staff knows that there is a chance to change the child.

Jesus is asking a question:
"Do you know how sick you really are?"

Most of the children in the dump have no idea how lost they are. They beg strangers for food but would be miserable if they were taken out of the dump and fed. They escape by sniffing glue, but few venture out of the dump into the town to truly escape. True change is possible only when they see the school on the edge of the dump and become curious about the better life it offers.

Many of us are like the children in the dump. We are begging for food or seeking momentary escape, but we don't even realize that we live in piles of garbage.

To us Jesus is asking a question: "Do you know how sick you really are?" Do you know you need to change—to grow?

DID I KNOW?

While recovering from the loss of our baby, I felt as if I had become a magnet for people in pain. I seemed to meet person after person who had experienced greater tragedies than mine. I remember telling a friend that I had never realized how much pain there is in the world.

She looked at me and said gently, "It was always there. You just couldn't see it."

In the months that followed, as I healed physically and emotionally, I felt a new kind of pain. It came from the realization that I had been unfeeling to the many people around me who had been suffering. I felt a deep sense of humiliation when I saw how much I had run away from people in pain. I had flashbacks of the many times I had tried to fix the problems people were experiencing instead of being an empathic friend who was willing to grieve with them. When a woman at work going through a difficult divorce had come in to talk, I had tried to help her think positively, encouraging her to get over it and move on.

What I began to see was how sick I really was. I had prayed to get over the pain of loss, but instead I saw that my need for healing was so much deeper than I had imagined. I began to pray and ask God to show me my own sickness and to help me sense other people's pain.

Perhaps for the first time in my life, I began to understand the meaning of grace as I saw how very needy I am. I began to realize just what a gift it is that Christ sees me as I really am and still loves me— even gave his life for me. No realization was more profound in my spiritual life. It is almost too much for me to absorb.

I began to pray and ask God to show me my own sickness and to help me sense other people's pain.

But in seeing what I could barely stand to look at, I realized that I could no longer go on the way I had been. The pain of change was not as great as the pain of remaining who I had been.

I was ready to say yes to the question "Do you know how sick you are?" and to a second question Jesus asks: "Do you want to get well?"

IS CHANGE POSSIBLE?

Let's say you know your sickness. Let's say you even want to change. But no matter how hard you try, you can't seem to change yourself. You want desperately to get control of yourself—manage your money wisely, stop overeating, avoid procrastination—but time after time you initiate change only to discover that it just doesn't stick.

The pain of change was not as great as the pain of remaining who I had been.

You may attempt an external action like joining Weight Watchers or setting up a budget, but when things get painful, you sabotage your own efforts. You say you want change, but you can't seem to commit to it. At the low point of your emotional roller-coaster ride, you give up and quit trying.

In his book *What You Can Change and What You Can't,* Dr. Martin Seligman discusses the various types of impulses, inclinations, and habits people want to change. After examining everything from therapy to medications, hypnosis to behavior modification, he concludes that there are simply things that people can't change about themselves.

Christian psychologist Chris Thurman puts it well when he says, "Personal power, as much as it gets held in high esteem in our culture, isn't enough to bring about deep, lasting change." He goes on to say that "lasting change takes place when the power source is strong enough to get it done."[1]

JOE'S FAILED EFFORTS

It took a man I'll call Joe nearly two decades to find that power source for lasting change. You see, Joe had been unable to walk for thirty-eight years. Maybe he'd been injured in an accident or had never recovered from a childhood disease. We don't know exactly how he came to be lame, but we do know it wasn't his only problem.

For years Joe had hung out at the pool at Bethesda in Jerusalem. Rumor had it that there was something special about the pool; every now and then an angel passed over, the water moved, and those who could get into the water were healed. Joe had seen the waters move. But by the time he dragged himself to the edge of the pool, it was calm again; he'd lost his chance to be healed.

Joe had his buddies at the pool—disabled like himself, coveting positions close to the water. They lay there, probably begging, sharing gossip, maybe taking bets on when the waters would move again. Those whose families brought them early in the morning or those who had seniority or were able to fend off the others laid their mats next to the pool. The less fortunate had spots out toward the gate.

One day a man visited the "magical" pool. The regulars welcomed tourists who threw money to the sick or offered them food. Sometimes they asked questions or touched the water. But this man walked through the crowd and looked directly at Joe as if he'd come just to see him. Joe searched his memory, trying to remember if he knew this man. Did he owe him money? There was something about the man that made him slightly uncomfortable.

The visitor seemed to know that Joe was an old-timer. Maybe he'd come to ask about someone who used to be at the pool or to hear a story about the water. Joe wondered if he should ask for money up front. Maybe he should try his more pathetic look and silently encourage an offering. But then this man did the most remarkable thing: He kneeled down, looked Joe right in the face, and asked, "Do you want to get well?"

What a stupid question, Joe thought with irritation. *Doesn't look like I'm going to get money out of this guy.* Still, he decided to go for sympathy. Maybe the guy was a do-gooder at heart. Joe cleared his throat, looked particularly helpless, and said, "I have no one to help me into the pool when the water is stirred." Nodding toward his useless legs, Joe continued, "While I am trying to get in, someone else goes down ahead of me." Joe glanced at the others, still making his dramatic point, when the man stood up, as if he were offended.

Joe stopped. Was the man going to hit him? No. With a gentle but firm voice, the man said, "Get up! Pick up your mat and walk."

Of course Joe knew he couldn't comply, but something about this man made Joe think he had better look as if he were trying. So he sat up. He pushed himself onto his knees. He stood. For the first time in thirty-eight years, his legs actually worked. He jumped up, picked up his mat, and immediately left the pool, the site of so many years of bad memories. He didn't turn back to see what had happened to the mysterious man.

As Joe was leaving the pool court, some official-looking men stopped him. They recognized him as a pool regular and were shocked to see him walking. But they also were surprised to see him carrying his rolled-up mat. After all, it was the Sabbath. Actually, they were more concerned about this violation of the Holy Day than about the healing. They looked at him accusingly, "The law forbids you to carry your mat."

Give me a break, guys, Joe wanted to say. But instead he assumed his pathetic look. "It's not my fault," he protested. "The man who made me well told me, 'Pick up your mat and walk.'" *I wasn't going to stick around and argue with that guy,* he wanted to add, but he thought better of it.

One of the officials nodded knowingly at the other. They didn't seem to be angry at Joe anymore.

Joe glanced toward the gate, eyeing his getaway path.

Suddenly the officials focused on him again. "Who is this fellow who told you to pick it up and walk?" There was no kindness in the voice.

Joe shrugged his shoulders. He had no idea who the guy was, and he didn't want any part of any hassle. Whatever beef these guys had was not his problem. After all, he had just been lying by the pool minding his own business when this thing started. The officials dismissed him with a wave of the hand, and Joe walked away, surprised that his legs were still moving.

Later, at the temple, a few people recognized him. "Hey, Joe, what's going on?"

"One minute I'm lying by the pool. The next I'm walking again. Must have been my lucky day." *No way am I telling them about the guy who healed me or those officials,* thought Joe. *I don't need that kind of trouble, just when I'm back on my feet again.*

A few minutes later he saw the man again. The healer. The guy who asked him the obvious question. The one in trouble with the law and the Sabbath lawyers. Joe hesitated, hoping he hadn't been seen. But again the guy walked right toward him. *Maybe I should tell him about those guys who are looking for him,* Joe thought.

But the man didn't seem to be concerned about anyone other than Joe. "You are well again," he said.

This guy has a knack for stating the obvious, Joe thought. *Of course I'm well. You were there.*

But then Joe looked, really looked at the guy for the first time. He saw the kind but serious eyes. The face that was both peaceful and purposeful. Joe was still afraid, but somehow he was attracted to this man. There was something special about him.

Before walking away, the man addressed Joe a final time: "Stop sinning or something worse may happen to you."

Joe shivered and knew that something had just happened to him that was more powerful than the poolside healing. This man had looked into Joe's soul; he had known that Joe was calling his healing "luck." This man had known that Joe was a cynic, a guy who had a hard time facing the truth.

But as Joe watched the man disappear in the crowd, he knew he had encountered Jesus. Jesus had made him well. And then Jesus had

changed him in a deeper, more profound way than a physical healing. He had broken down the walls and healed his hardened soul.
"What was that all about?" one of his buddies no doubt asked.

This time Joe wasn't even tempted to respond with a smart
comeback. "It was Jesus," he said. "Jesus healed me."

*Jesus had changed him in a deeper,
more profound way than a physical healing.*

He saw the officials again, the ones who had accused him of
working on the Sabbath. "It was Jesus," he said excitedly. "He was the
one who healed me." He didn't stop long enough to hear their
response. He was too busy telling everyone he encountered, "I was
lying by the pool of Bethesda when Jesus came and healed me!"

WHOSE PLAN?

The story of the man healed at the pool of Bethesda is recorded
in John 5:1–15.

When I've read this story, I've sometimes been judgmental about
this man I've called Joe. Jesus miraculously healed him, yet his
response was first to whine and then to be ungrateful. Jesus had to
go back and remind the guy that he'd experienced a miracle.

Yet now as I read this passage over again, I see myself in Joe.
What about you?

We know we want things to change—we know we want to get
off the dump—but we have our own plans for how that will happen.

Instead of praying "Thy will be done," we try to tell God what
his will for us should be.

How often do we have our problems all figured out—the unfairness, the circumstances beyond our control, the heredity or family
problems that we are stuck with. We know them so well that they
sometimes become a badge for us, an identity that gives us comfort
in our world. "I am codependent" or "I am the child of an alcoholic"
are painful—and breakthrough—realizations, but they can become
excuses to keep us from growing or changing. Worse, they can blind
us to what God has in mind for us.

TWO HARD QUESTIONS

Instead of praying "Thy will be done,"
we try to tell God what his will for us should be.

The disabled man at the pool had spent a great deal of time — years — thinking about his problem, positioning himself close to the water's edge, scheming: If only he could get into the water, his troubles would be over. But Jesus had bigger plans for him. The man was so obsessed with his plan for recovery that he didn't even hear the offer of a miracle.

"Do you want to get well?" is a question God is asking each of us. The answer isn't easy. We may be seeing a qualified Christian counselor or psychologist. We may understand that we eat out of a desire to be loved or that we are obsessed with the opposite sex because of what was lacking in our childhood. We may have read every recovery book on the shelf and be able to discuss in detail our reactions to circumstances around us.

Dr. Martin Seligman, in the first chapter of his book *What You Can Change and What You Can't,* says:

> Millions are struggling to change: We diet, we jog, we meditate. We adopt new modes of thought to counteract our depressions. We practice relaxation to curtail stress. . . . Sometimes it works. But distressingly often, self-improvement and psychotherapy fail. The cost is enormous. We think we are worthless. We feel guilty and ashamed. We believe we have no willpower and that we are failures. We give up trying to change.[2]

So what is the answer? Should we give up and let nature take its course? Should we simply say, "This is who I am; take it or leave it"? If only human options were available, that might be the course to take. But as Christians we are promised more. Jesus asks, "Do you want to get well?" He doesn't ask, "Do you want to help me move you through recovery?" What he is speaking about is true change. Jesus can heal us.

For anyone who has joined Alcoholics Anonymous or has taken part in a Twelve Step program based on the A.A. model, it is clear that part of the reason this program has been so successful is that it is based on more than human willpower and understanding. The Twelve Steps of Alcoholics Anonymous are as follows:

1. We admitted we were powerless over alcohol—that our lives had become unmanageable.
2. Came to believe that a Power greater than ourselves could restore us to sanity.
3. Made a decision to turn our will and our lives over to the care of God as we understood him.
4. Made a searching and fearless moral inventory of ourselves.
5. Admitted to God, to ourselves, and to another human being the exact nature of our wrongs.
6. Were entirely ready to have God remove all these defects of character.
7. Humbly asked him to remove our shortcomings.
8. Made a list of all persons we had harmed and became willing to make amends to them all.
9. Made direct amends to such people wherever possible, except when to do so would injure them or others.
10. Continued to take personal inventory and when we were wrong promptly admitted it.
11. Sought through prayer and meditation to improve our conscious contact with God as we understood him, praying only for knowledge of his will for us and the power to carry that out.
12. Having had a spiritual awakening as the result of these steps, we tried to carry this message to alcoholics and to practice these principles in all our affairs.[3]

To read this creed in the original form is to realize that the alcoholic has heard Jesus' question and responded, "Yes, I want to get well." He or she takes responsibility for actions. There is no whining or accusing. There are no more "if onlys." There is a giving up of excuses and self-improvement formulas and personal plans. Will and life are turned over to God with the humble but faith-filled words, "Yes, I want to get well."

Many good things have come from the so-called recovery movement. Many people have for the first time realized the nature of their problems. But many have become stuck in recovery. They are caught in an endless cycle of understanding without movement. They can, like the man at the pool of Bethesda, give every reason why they are not better.

*To get well—to change—is terribly frightening
and threatening.*

But Jesus did not talk about recovery. He preached the gospel of change. He did not offer to help the man into the waters or use his power to keep others from going ahead of him. He did not even acknowledge that the man had placed his hope in a superstitious pagan ritual of the day. He simply offered him a miracle.

So often we are so stuck in our ruts that we decorate their sides and nestle into a safe place to spend the rest of our lives. To get well—to change—is terribly frightening and threatening.

Even worse, we become so preoccupied with our ruts that we do not see the bigger picture. Our own course of change can become a dump of its own, as if our rut were located in a bigger trench. All we can think about is crawling a few feet but never getting out of the trench. And yet God sees that we are in much greater trouble than being in our simple rut.

*True change comes as Christ works
his inner work in our lives.*

When Jesus healed the man at the pool of his physical problem, he also gave him the opportunity to be made well spiritually. But the man had focused so long on his physical need and his own plans for healing that he missed the greatest gift Jesus offered. It was only later at the temple that the man became well. Until then he had never realized how sick he *really* was.

True change does not happen by simply buying an organizer or stocking the refrigerator with new food or setting up a new filing system. It does not come with a doctor's medication or under a surgeon's knife. Psychology or medicine alone has never been successful at finding a formula for change that leads to wholeness of spirit.

True change comes as Christ works his inner work in our lives. I previously quoted Dr. Chris Thurman: "Lasting change takes place when the power source is strong enough to get it done." Let me end this chapter by finishing his thought: "and only one power source is capable of bringing about deep permanent change: God."

QUESTIONS FOR REFLECTION

1. Are there people you know who seem incapable of change? Do you think they are unwilling or unable to let God work in their lives?
2. What situations in your life are recurring problems? Have you asked God to show you what the underlying issues really are?
3. Do you really want to get well? Have you asked God to heal you from the difficult struggles in your life? Do you believe he can really make you well?
4. Have you sought the help of a Christian counselor to help you understand your problems?

Chapter Six

THE MYTH OF CONTROL

O n Pentecost Sunday of 1994, I sat in church feeling anxious and confused. For nearly fourteen years I had run my own magazine publishing company. We had been financially stable, I had wonderful employees, and I enjoyed being an entrepreneur. But things had begun to change. One of my oldest clients was having a hard time paying our bills. Months were going by without payment for work we had already completed. Another client had decided to close a magazine because of the rising costs of paper and postage. And my landlord announced a rent increase.

I knew I had two choices: I could work harder to replace the clients we were losing and to pay the bills that were mounting up, or I could cut back, reduce expenses, and run a smaller company. I began to pray that God would show me what course to take.

Meanwhile, one of our newest clients was asking for more and more of my time. I was resisting, but I was intrigued by the work that would take me out of magazines and into new areas of media. But it didn't seem to make any sense. My background was in magazines. At forty I was feeling too old to move into a different field altogether. Besides, I knew what I was doing in the magazine world. If I started all over again I would lose the security I had.

When the sermon began, I tried hard to listen. I assumed the preacher would go into the typical discussion of gifts initiated at Pentecost. I had heard it before, and I was beginning to wonder why I had even come to church that morning. But then the preacher caught my attention. He talked about the first "acts" recorded in the Acts of the Apostles and the desire of the disciples to control the ongoing ministry started when Jesus walked among them. He showed how they carefully chose Mathias to replace Judas. And then he talked about the incredible disruption caused by Pentecost. "Do you know how you can tell if the Spirit of God is at work?" he asked rhetorically.

The movement of the Spirit is unexpected and uncontrolled by human logic.

I held my breath, waiting for his answer. "Things won't happen the way you expect them to," he said. "The movement of the Spirit is unexpected and uncontrolled by human logic. It will surprise you, maybe even disrupt your plans."

I let my breath out and silently thanked God for speaking to me so directly. *Let go of your grip. Let go of your need to control your life.* On one level—conventional human wisdom—taking this job didn't make sense. But God had once again reminded me that I could trust him, even if my human instincts resisted letting go. It was as if he had added, *Turn toward the wind, and then sit back and let me show you where we can go together.*

Later I began to read my devotions from the book *My Utmost for His Highest.* The text was Matthew 6:25 (KJV): "Take no thought for your life, what ye shall eat, or what ye shall drink; nor yet for your body what ye shall put on." Oswald Chambers says that "common-sense carefulness in a disciple [is] infidelity." When a believer begins to think "I will not trust what I cannot see, that is where infidelity begins." He concludes with these words: "The great word of Jesus to his disciples is *abandon.*"

Abandon. From a human perspective, the word is terrifying. Everything in us says *hold on.* But Chambers' point is well taken. When we hold on to earthly, human security we are being unfaithful to God. We are denying that we believe what we claim to believe. We say we have faith, but we mean that we have faith in God and in ourselves, instead of faith in God alone.

Even the will to give in and let God take control takes divine intervention. *Help me stay out of your way. Keep me from clinging to human security,* I have to pray, just to get myself to the point of wanting to turn my life over to God each day.

HOLDING ON

We have so many layers of control that we hardly even recognize them. And understandably so.

When my sixty-four-year-old father learned that his brain cancer had reappeared, robbing him of the hope of years or even months, he didn't cry or scream or despair. Instead he left the doctor's office, went home, and did something totally in keeping with his character: He cleaned out his closet.

He carefully amassed piles to go to the Salvation Army. Other things he threw out. He kept only the few clothes he would need for the days he had left. It was Dad's way of making sure that no one else would be left with the task of cleaning up after him. It was also his way of controlling what little he could.

My friend Lynne had a similar reaction when her husband of twenty-three years came home one evening and announced that he had been living a lie and was leaving her to marry the true love of his life, his secretary. Lynne listened calmly to his words, did the dinner dishes, and began defrosting the freezer. By the time her husband was finished packing, she had turned on the self-cleaning oven and was washing and waxing the floor. "I know it sounds crazy now," she says, "but I wanted him to walk out remembering that I'd always been a good homemaker."

Psychologists tell us that denial is often our first reaction when we are faced with tragedy.

My father and my friend both reacted to devastating news with strangely normal behavior. They were probably in shock or denial or both. Psychologists tell us that denial is often our first reaction when we are faced with tragedy. It's as if the mind says, *If I don't admit this is happening, it will go away.* This reaction is a somewhat normal defense mechanism. It becomes abnormal when a person continues to refuse to speak of difficulties long after the event. That refusal to deal with reality can lead to deep psychological and spiritual problems.

Says noted psychologist Larry Crabb, "For many Christians, denial has become a habit. Chronic denial as a means of coping leads to stiffness and rigidity.... People who deny how they really feel typically are unable to enter and touch another person's life deeply."[1]

When faced with circumstances out of our control, we often react by controlling what we can. It is typically a temporary reaction, like denial. But if we continue to be obsessive about controlling what we can, we develop not only psychological problems but also spiritual ones as well. Says Crabb, "Fallen man would prefer to keep control of his own destiny, though he is impotent, rather than trusting in the 'uncertainty' of a faithful and good God."[2]

When unwelcome change blows into our lives, it upends us in disconcerting ways. Psychologists Gerald Richardson and Judson Swihart compare the effects of crisis to a triangle turned from a stable base to its unstable point. "Within a matter of weeks a triangle [a person in crisis] will fall back onto its base again. But it will not land at the same place on the plane as it previously was. It will move in one of two directions: toward growth and better functioning or toward dysfunction."[3]

When I speak to audiences about change, I often start by asking, "How do you react when you hear the word *change*?" Recently one uninhibited listener pulled her jean-covered legs up to her chest, wrapped her arms around her knees, tucked her head down, and assumed a fetal position. She got a laugh from the crowd for aptly demonstrating what is the typical response many of us feel.

WE VALUE CONTROL

We are creatures who value control. We want to know what we can depend on and what we can't. When product claims are false, we sue. We have developed dozens of agencies just to regulate communication, air travel, health, and education. Yet as any frustrated air traveler knows, the Federal Aviation Administration can assure us of a refund if our flight is canceled, but it cannot protect us from the thunderstorm that comes between us and our important meeting half a continent away. Just when we think we have some sense of control over our lives, we realize how foolish we are to think we have any control at all.

Just when we think we have some sense of control over our lives, we realize how foolish we are to think we have any control at all.

The winter of 1994 set records in many states for its brutality. In my normally mild part of the country, the public schools closed twelve days for snow or ice conditions, when even one snow day is a rarity in a typical winter. East coast cities ran out of sand and road salt. In New York City, a box of table salt cost fourteen dollars during the height of the crisis. In Washington, D.C., offices were ordered closed for one day due to a shortage of power caused by the *cold*, let alone snow.

After the first week or two of these conditions, people became almost fatalistic. Some refused to go out, even when the roads were clear and there wasn't a cloud in the sky. Some made arrangements—contingent on the weather or back-up plans. Schools issued updates on how long classes would continue into the summer. My children watched weather reports and no longer hoped for snow, knowing that another day of school closings meant a shorter summer vacation. From December through March, we had little control—and we felt uneasy throughout the season.

WHY WE SEEK CONTROL

It all started in the Garden of Eden, of course. Adam and Eve in the idyllic setting. No restraints, no concerns, no pollution, no wars. How could Satan hope to compete?

Satan offered Eve the very same type of temptation he offers us each day. He offered her a chance to control her destiny. She could be an independent creature. He probably explained to her how much it would help God if she could make her own decisions. After all, she and Adam were so dependent on God. Wouldn't it be better for all of them if the first couple began to pull their own weight? Satan even told Eve that their relationship with God would be more interesting to him if Adam and Eve were more like God. It must be boring for God to maintain the relationship with such dependent creatures.

As Chambers puts it, "The good is always the enemy of the best." Eve reasoned that taking a bite of the forbidden fruit would be a good thing to do. She took her eyes off the Best and fell right into Satan's trap.

Eve, knowing that the subtleties would probably be lost on Adam, took matters into her own hands. She knew there was a risk that disobeying God would cause problems, but she thought she could probably handle them. Even before she ate the fruit from the forbidden tree, she was making her plans.

It probably took just one bite for Eve to understand that she had power. Adam was no match for her. By the time she seduced him into taking a bite, she probably seemed almost God-like to him. She had a new confidence and insight that he wanted, too. She was decisive, strong, directed. She had the false bravado so often seen in flailing humans.

We believe that we have the knowledge to choose our destiny.
꩜

Eve started it. Adam went along for the ride. And each of us, to a greater or lesser extent, has bought into the myth of control. We believe that we have the knowledge to choose our destiny. We have Filofaxes to plot our lives, computer programs to analyze our investments, and personal trainers to monitor our fitness. Every day we mimic the infamous line of Alexander Haig just after President Reagan had been shot: "I am in control." And we sound just as foolish as he did. As the old Hebrew saying goes: "Man plans; God laughs."

The more sure we are of ourselves, the less God can work on us. The firmer we become, the less God can change us. The more we value control, the more devastated we will be by the inevitable blow to our carefully constructed lives. The more we pick ourselves up and go right back to calling the shots, the less we will be able to learn from the changes that come our way.

We live busy lives, full of pieces that seem to threaten to fly in all directions at any moment. We have carpools and deadlines and lawns to mow. As Corrie ten Boom said, "If the devil can't make us bad, he will make us busy."[4] When we're busy, we don't just ignore God; we make control our god. We schedule and organize and get more and more efficient.

When we're busy, we don't just ignore God;
we make control our god.
꩜

But God doesn't want us efficient. As uncomfortable as it is to contemplate, God wants us vulnerable and open, not controlled and secure. I don't mean that he wants us to exhibit the characteristics of human insecurity. He does not want us to be fidgety and self-conscious.

Instead, he wants us to be at peace, secure in the knowledge that he has our future in his hands.

Why do we resist moving toward God when things are going well in our lives—when we feel as if we are in control?

Perhaps it is because we believe that moving from what we have to what we don't see or understand represents a loss of what we hold most dear, including our identity, our relationships, and our security.

THE FEAR OF LOSING IDENTITY

We live in a society obsessed with identity. Who I am is defined by my title, my accomplishments, my house, and even my children. Sadly, even the church has given some personalities celebrity status, with authors, recording artists, radio preachers, and television hosts being set apart as special.

But the Bible clearly indicates that as Christians our identity rests only in Christ; any one of us is no better or worse than any other sinner redeemed by God's grace. As we understand this, giving up a title or a platform is a small price to pay for moving closer to God.

A friend of mine was a well-known author and singer until she stepped away from the spotlight, much to the shock of her agent, publisher, and producer. While in the spotlight, she was frequently called by various power brokers of the Christian world, who wanted her to appear on magazine covers, to host award banquets, and to write books. Now her phone rings only occasionally since she is living a quiet life of study and reflection. When I had lunch with her recently she looked happy, relaxed, and at peace. "I wouldn't trade what I have now for any of what I left behind," she said. "It is a terrible trap we get into when we let other people define who we are. We have to help the church see that it is a mistake to set anyone up as being more than anyone else."

An identity abandoned for the sake of following Christ need not be seen as a loss. "I can hardly say the word," my friend Julie confessed over the phone. "I am going to be a *missionary*," she said with a giggle. "It's the last thing in the world I would have thought I would ever be, but now I can't wait." Julie didn't set out to go to the mission field. She only sought to follow Christ more closely and use her talents for him. It was quite a shock when she and her husband were offered the opportunity to work in Germany and Eastern Europe. It

TURN TOWARD THE WIND

seemed so right that neither of them could believe it. Julie is using her talents as an editor, while her husband uses his teaching and preaching skills. It is the ideal career opportunity as well as the perfect situation for them to grow spiritually. Julie doesn't identify with the word *missionary* because of the expectations she had of people who served in missions. Yet Julie couldn't be happier than in the role in which God has placed her. When she was willing to give up control of her identity, she found her identity in Christ.

For me, the notion of giving up my company and moving into a related but different field meant a loss of identity. When I took my new job and gave up my own company, I entered a field where no one knew my name or my reputation. Instead of getting phone calls quickly returned, I had to leave detailed messages explaining who I was and why I was calling. When I proposed a course of action, people no longer trusted me because they knew what I had accomplished. I had to explain everything from scratch. There were days when I felt frustrated. But even in the difficult times, I knew I was growing. And because of the way God had revealed his plan for me, I knew I was where I was supposed to be.

THE FEAR OF CHANGING RELATIONSHIPS

We are often afraid that following Christ will mean a loss of relationships. And sometimes it does.

One of the goals of Alcoholics Anonymous is to help recovering alcoholics find new, healthier relationships. It is often difficult to stay "on the wagon" when friends—still drinking—want the alcoholic to join them for a cocktail. It is hard to give up the camaraderie of drunkenness for the stark reality of sobriety. As the popular television show *Cheers* demonstrated, bars can be places "where everyone knows your name" and "where they're always glad you came." A bar scene can also be a "dump" to which people cling instead of dealing with the true issues.

Changing patterns can often threaten friends. People who join AA can be ridiculed by drinking friends who insist drinking is not a problem. If one person admits his or her drinking is out of hand, others may have to confront their problems too.

70

*At times we have to move from what we know
to what we do not know; from what is seen to what is unseen.*

It is not uncommon for a spouse to be pleased at the weight loss of a husband or wife and then to begin to sabotage the attempts when the spouse consciously or subconsciously realizes that the nature of the marital relationship will change. Others will notice how attractive the person is. Overtly or not, the question may become, *What's an attractive woman like her doing with him?*

To move closer to God can be confusing, even to other believers. We are sometimes personally called to take a path that does not make sense to others. Sometimes a walk of faith cannot be explained at all. At times we have to move from what we know to what we do not know; from what is seen to what is unseen. It is a step of faith that may seem like a contradiction to those looking at standards set by the world.

THE FEAR OF LOSING SECURITY

Another idol of our modern society is security. There is nothing wrong with providing for our families and saving for retirement in hopes that we won't become a burden to others. At the same time, a healthy abandonment to God and his care realizes that the security we receive from insurance, pensions, and savings plans is all temporal.

Over the past years people have been shocked to discover that companies can close down guaranteed pension plans, insurance companies can fail, and even savings and loans can shut their doors with our money inside. It is wise to be prudent. But it is foolhardy to place all of our trust in human institutions.

Last year Charles Colson received the million dollar Templeton prize for Progress in Religion. Colson was obviously moved but also saw the great irony in the award. As he told a small gathering of friends and Prison Fellowship board members: "Twenty years ago I was a hotshot lawyer who had all kinds of ideas about how to be successful. In my wildest dreams, I never would have believed that someone would award me such a prestigious and generous prize for being a failure and an ex-convict who spends his time with other prisoners."

God's economy is different from ours. He must shake his head as we desperately hold on to jobs, scurry to find better savings rates, lay awake at night wondering how we will pay the bills. Jesus' words of Matthew 11:28–30 stand in contrast to our frenzy:

> Come to me, all you who are weary and burdened, and I will give you rest. Take my yoke upon you and learn from me, for I am gentle and humble in heart, and you will find rest for your souls. For my yoke is easy and my burden is light.

Jesus is saying that coming to him will not hurt our need for security but will give us a security that supersedes anything we have known. The Christian life is not a life of security in what we have but in what we believe. Our faith is "being sure of what we hope for and certain of what we do not see" (Heb. 11:1).

And a basic tenet of that belief system is that our goal in this life is to become more and more like Christ. That process runs counter to every success formula known on earth. It does not need security or the status quo. It surprises people with its seeming audacity and ability to seek the truth in the midst of chaos.

The Christian life is not a life of security in what we have but in what we believe.

Perhaps the best way to illustrate this is to tell the story of little Hannah Clem and her mother, Kelly. On Palm Sunday 1994, Hannah was attending the Goshen United Methodist Church in Piedmont, Alabama, where her mother is a pastor. Hannah was preparing to give her part in the church's Easter pageant, but actually she became part of a pageant more holy than anything she or the congregation could have imagined.

Unknown to any of the people gathered that Sunday, a tornado was spinning toward their church. As the children stood ready to present their program, the tornado crashed into the church, bringing the roof down on the entire congregation. Little Hannah, full of life one moment, was killed instantly. Her mother was battered and bruised and then devastated by the grief of losing her daughter.

During the next week, reports of the tragedy were carried by the media. This story would have been lost among the many other tragedies of the world except for one thing: Hannah's mother believed in God and had a faith that transcended coping. With her face battered and often streaked with tears, Kelly Clem proclaimed to the media and to the congregation that Jesus Christ could redeem even this great tragedy.

A few said she was in denial. Others suggested shock. But some saw what Katie Couric, the cohost of the *Today* show, named: "What incredible faith."

Kelly Clem never denied that her heart was broken or that she wouldn't mourn forevermore the loss of her beautiful four-year-old daughter. And she didn't blame God for the tragedy. She spoke firmly to the belief that God does not want little children in Easter dresses to die.

But she did say that God's grace is greater than the horror. She moved beyond her personal agony to a superhuman level, comforting mourners in her community and proclaiming to the nation that God is not dead; Christ is risen indeed. Throughout Holy Week broadcasts around the world carried the story of this little church in Alabama and the minister/mother who still believed in God.

Tornadoes happen every spring. So do floods and fires and man-made disasters. Usually they get a quick mention on the news. After all, tragedy happens. But rarely is such great faith found in the ashes of despair.

Kelly Clem is a woman of God who was willing to be used by him even in her darkest moment. I expect she would say that her testimony of faith—her foundation of security—came not because she had been well-schooled in doctrine or knew the importance of the media presentation. By all accounts, Kelly had been a changed woman long before tragedy struck. Deep in her heart she knew that there are no promises in this life. Yet she completely believes in the promise of life to come. It is not a belief that is rehearsed or controlled. It is a faith that comes from a deep understanding of grace.

I watched day after day as this woman proclaimed her faith on national television and I prayed, "Give me that kind of faith, Lord." Of course I prayed that I could learn this lesson without any physical harm coming to my children, but I asked God to cut no corners when it came to my own growth. I had gone from a love of the secure to an understanding that my life as a Christian had to be about change—about giving up the false sense of control I had over the winds of change.

THE GREAT ADVENTURE

We resist change because change almost always means lack of control. Even when change is for the better, it is a disruption of comfortable patterns. We feel as if the ground is shifting, the "givens" are gone, and our future is unknown. We cannot dream, only dread what will come next. We feel insecure and abandoned. And that is just when God can work best in our lives and hearts.

What is most amazing is that the more we give in and let God take over, the more our fear of change moves to anticipation. Steven Curtis Chapman summed it up with his award-winning song "The Great Adventure." God is taking us on a great adventure. It will be out of our power and control. And it will be a ride like none we would have planned for ourselves. As we loosen our grip on the reins of our own lives, he is directing us down a trail we have never known.

QUESTIONS FOR REFLECTION

1. In what ways do you value control in your own life? How have you fought to maintain control even in the midst of tragedy or disruption?
2. How do you respond to the idea that the Holy Spirit may be at work disrupting your plans?
3. Can you think of times in your life when things didn't go the way you had planned, but you later realized that things turned out better than what you had planned?
4. How do you define yourself? How important are each of the labels you wear? What would happen if you could no longer use one of these labels?
5. What makes you feel secure? How would you respond if you could no longer count on those things?

Chapter Seven

REVERSAL OF FORTUNE

W hen we step back from control, we also step back from power. Power is one of the most important human currencies—the ability to have access, respect, and dominance. Without it we are at the mercy of others. We no longer make the rules; we play by someone else's. Power is beloved by people in business and in religion. It rears its head at PTA meetings and in boardrooms, on the floor of the Senate and in the sandbox on a playground. With power we have control, and with control we have the sense that we can determine our destiny.

But of course, power is a trap, just as control is a delusion. It becomes obvious when the CEO of a major corporation, having jockeyed for power, beat out his rivals, and emerged all-powerful, is suddenly felled by a heart attack. Or when a merger is announced and the man at the top is the last person anyone wants around the new company.

One of the most amazing understandings of power was displayed in South Africa in 1994 when President F. W. deKlerck willingly opened the country's election to all citizens of the country, knowing that the black majority would surely gain power and vote him out of office. After the election was over and Nelson Mandela was elected the nation's first black president, Mandela demonstrated that he had learned many lessons during his imprisonment and in his fight for equality. Instead of seizing power and trying to humiliate the former government, he thanked deKlerck and accepted his new post humbly. He seemed to be saying by his actions, *We will not make the same mistakes of those who came before us.*

Power is one of the most important human currencies.
Without it we are at the mercy of others.

～❦　❧～

Lee Atwater is another example of a man of power who learned lessons of humility.

WHEN LOSS MEANS GAIN

Lee Atwater was twenty minutes late for the breakfast meeting at which he was the scheduled speaker, but he strolled in without apology, grinning broadly and shaking hands with the people he passed. He bounded up to the podium, rescuing the somewhat embarrassed master of ceremonies and drawled out a greeting to the audience.

Most of us gathered at the early meeting were drinking coffee in a desperate attempt to wake up, but Lee looked as if he'd never been drowsy in his life. He moved from side to side at the podium, unable to control the energy that pulsed through him. He was charismatic, amusing, cynical, and arrogant. He peppered his talk with colorful language and unapologetically named people who stood in the way of "progress." By the time he bounded off the platform half an hour later to run to another gathering, all of us were exhausted. We felt as if a tornado had blown through the gathering.

My encounter with Lee Atwater was typical of the man. He swept through Washington in the late 1980s with a youthful energy and confidence that was most often described as "cocky." He was a brilliant strategist and political adviser who was credited with winning the 1988 election for George Bush. But he was more than that. The *Washington Post* often carried stories of Atwater sightings at local blues clubs where he played his guitar into the wee hours. Then he'd be seen jogging beside the president just after dawn. His zest for life and ability to seize every moment was legendary. So was his chutzpah.

Although he worked for a man most known for polite and gracious consensus building, Atwater didn't seem to care who he offended. Many of his comments on political opponents were unquotable in mixed company, a combination of southern homespun humor and urbane nastiness. People either loved him or hated him. And there were plenty of people in both camps. Nothing seemed to slow him down, and each day in Washington brought him more friends and enemies. He was once pictured in his office with a phone at either ear, while directing someone running from his office on an appointed errand.

Then one day while Atwater was giving one of his trademark speeches, he began to shake uncontrollably. He was rushed to a hospital, where doctors examined the dynamo and soon delivered troubling news: Atwater had a brain tumor. Malignant. Inoperable. Certainly fatal. Washington was shocked. It had seemed that nothing could slow this man, yet disease had stopped him in his tracks.

After seeing his lean face in the papers as he jogged, gave a campaign speech, or jammed with his guitar, I was shocked months later when Atwater was pictured—his face swollen from the steroids that kept his tumor under control but stole his trademark energy and good looks. Lee Atwater, formerly one of the most powerful and least vulnerable—and most "under control" people in the world, now faced a precarious future.

Over the months another story emerged. Political enemies were receiving notes from Atwater. Most were apologies. Some contained confessions of sins they would never have known Atwater committed. When interviewed, Atwater quoted less from his typical favorites, Machiavelli and *The Art of War,* and more from the Bible.

A newspaper article that appeared eight months after his diagnosis was titled "Religion Changes 'Bad Boy' of Politics" and included this summary:

> Republican National Committee chairman Lee Atwater, once branded the "pit bull of American politics," is a changed man.
>
> "I have found Jesus Christ. It's that simple," he said in an interview this week. "He's made a difference, and I'm glad I've found him while there's still time."[1]

To cynical Washington, the conversion came as quite a shock. No one had been more irreverent than Atwater. No one would have been more likely to ridicule a person who spoke openly of his faith. It was as if the conversion of Saul had found a modern-day embodiment.

The notes continued to arrive in the mailboxes of former political foes and even fellow party loyalists with whom Atwater had competed for positions and power. Many people were more uncomfortable with the changed attitude than with the now unrecognizable appearance. Some openly wondered if the tumor had affected his mind, bringing on religious delusions.

Many people were more uncomfortable with the changed attitude than with the now unrecognizable appearance.

⚜   ⚜

In February 1991, less than a year after his collapse, grotesque pictures of Atwater appeared in *Life* magazine along with a first-person account of his illness and his coming to faith. As a friend of mine who knew Lee personally observed: "That Lee would allow pictures of his swollen face and disabled body to appear in a national magazine shows how humble he has become. His image, his strength, his high energy persona were all very important to Lee."

His funeral two months later was held in the Washington National Cathedral, the only D.C. church large enough to accommodate the mourners. In the eulogy, the Reverend William A. Holmes summed up Atwater's life and death:

> [He] left a rare legacy.... the truth that winning a campaign isn't worth what you lose if winning is the pinnacle of what you live for.
>
> During the last year of his life, the Christian faith defined how he understood himself in relationship with God, and in relationship with other human beings. The wondrous irony of his death is that a brain tumor, which eventually took away his life, was also the occasion of his being more and more alive to what life is all about.[2]

The *Washington Post*, reporting on the funeral, defined Atwater's life as a "paradox." Perhaps no word better describes what happened to Atwater or Saul or any who begin to understand and live Jesus' call to abandonment, recorded in Mark 8:35: "For whoever wants to save his life will lose it, but whoever loses his life for me and for the gospel will save it."

THE "THREAT" OF INTERNAL CHANGE

When the world talks about change, it is usually a visible, tangible change. Weight is lost, a career takes a new course, a move is made. But spiritual change is a shifting of attitude, mindset, internal priorities. Pride is replaced with humility. A success orientation disappears. God and people become more important than things. These changes are threatening to many people—even people who are religious.

*These changes are threatening to many people
—even people who are religious.*

In Jesus' day it was threatening, too. The Pharisees had power and control. It was part of what made them so closed to the message Christ brought—a message that called for a reversal of order: The strong to become weak and the weak strong. That hard word threatened the Pharisees and made perfect sense to those who had the ears to hear. Jesus said, "Follow me and give up control and power and their accompanying security." By "saving their lives," the Pharisees—religious leaders who couldn't imagine life without power and control—lost their lives. To them religion had become a way to use power and control over the people. They had their rituals, their institutions, their hierarchy. Along came Jesus with a message that was simple and totally excluded the need for their laws and their positions. From the time he began his ministry, those with power looked for ways to destroy him.

A few years ago, a talented woman I knew became a Christian after living a glamorous and hedonistic life. With the excitement of a new convert, she wanted to use the gifts she had by pursuing employment with a Christian organization; full of naive enthusiasm, she went to work for a large ministry. In one of her first meetings on staff, she heard a debate about an industry practice that sounded somewhat unethical to her. Not wanting to sound judgmental, she asked a carefully worded question that she thought appropriate: "What would Jesus do?"

To her dismay, her question was met with raised eyebrows and nervous coughs. Finally the head of the organization looked at her and said pointedly, "That's a very good question philosophically, but we have an organization to run here. We need to know how to maximize our impact."

Concern about the impact and a deeper concern about worldly security was the last thing this woman expected to hear in a Christian organization. Disillusioned, she left and went back to work in her former company.

UNSEEN ISSUES

As Christians we are called daily to abandon control, power, and security—to become more like Christ. This process is nearly impossible to see or measure. It is an intangible movement out of which we manifest attitudes such as love, joy, peace, gentleness, patience, goodness, and humility. The great mystery is that we cannot make any of these virtues a goal in themselves or they are simply legalistic disciplines. If they grow out of an inner change, they are responses that come from the heart and soul. We are not martyrs when we love the unlovable. We are people with a deep appreciation of our own unlovableness. As we understand the grace that is given to us, we are able to offer grace to others.

> *As Christians we are called daily to abandon control, power, and security.*
>
> ❧ ❧

I am intrigued by how many times the word *see* appears in the Bible as a directive. We read it in Isaiah 43:19: "See, I am doing a new thing!" It appears in the John 5 account of the man we called Joe. "See, you are well again" (v. 14). It is as if we need a constant reminder to look at what God is doing in us as we allow him to work in us.

For Lee Atwater, it took a brain tumor and a complete loss of power to see what was truly important. Such human tragedies are often the occasion of turning to God because they strip us of all that is humanly dear. For a man I knew professionally, it took the death of a son, the victim of a rare, fatal disease.

FROM PRESTIGE TO REAL POWER

The father, an impressive, born leader, was a well-known speaker and author and had often been placed in powerful positions of authority. His son also had many of the same characteristics. He excelled in college sports, graduated with honors from an Ivy League school, and was embarking on a promising career when he was struck down by the disease that sapped him of his strength and finally his life.

The man was devastated by the loss of his child. *Why would God take someone with such promise?* he wondered. Instead of his usual powerful demeanor, the man often broke down in public. He stepped aside from some of his public positions. Instead of leading the groups in which he was a member, he became quiet, even withdrawn. He cried out to God in anger and frustration.

And then slowly, people noticed something different about this man. He listened to others in a new way. His speaking was less about leadership and more about servanthood. He passed by opportunities that once would have excited him.

This man who had once focused on power and prestige had changed. People saw it. They didn't talk about the fact that he sometimes wiped a tear from his eye in a meeting as much as they noted that he didn't seem as concerned about power. They noted that he looked out for others more than himself.

This great man who had accomplished so much through power and success was accomplishing even more through humility and pain. He had become what Henri Nouwen calls a "wounded healer." Says Nouwen: "A Christian community is … a healing community not because wounds are cured and pains are alleviated, but because wounds and pains become openings or occasions for a new vision. Mutual confession then becomes a mutual deepening of hope, and sharing weakness becomes a reminder to one and all of the coming strength."[3]

In his pain, this man had learned what it felt like to be lonely, hurt, and treated unfairly. All of his accomplishments were worthless when it came to saving his son's life. In this realization, he was able to identify with the pain of those around him—and that became his strength. He no longer made light of others' hardships. He understood them for the first time.

It was a great tragedy that he had lost his son. But it would have been an even greater tragedy if he hadn't been willing to let God use the loss to change him.

It is as if God is asking us to enter a long, dark tunnel. He promises that we will see clearly once we emerge on the other side, but for a time we must step out in faith, enter the tunnel, and leave behind all that we know. God promises that once we come out the other end of the tunnel we will never want to go back. Lee Atwater, Chuck Colson, the father who lost his son—all affirm that this is true. But taking the first few steps into what is unseen, with the brightly lit world at our backs, is the most difficult move to make. It requires faith and obedience and offers only the clear promise: "See, I am doing a new thing."

QUESTIONS FOR REFLECTION

1. How are you enticed by power? Do you enjoy using it in the workplace, the home, your community?
2. What do you fear about loss of power or control?
3. Have you seen people in your church or in another religious organization threatened by change? Is their resistance based on biblical principles?
4. How often do you ask the question, "What would Jesus do?"
5. As you take a hard look at your life, are you willing to trust God and give up control?

Chapter Eight

*F*ACING THE GOOD, THE BAD, AND THE UGLY

C hange happens. That it happens to us is a surprise only at the first great disruption. But that it happens *in* us is a mystery more profound than birth or death or life itself. Change happens in us not because we will it, but because we give up our will. It happens not according to plans but when our own plans are laid on the altar. It happens not because we deserve it but because we are humiliated by how undeserving we are. It happens most often through the clarifying vacuum of tragedy, but it also happens when the good times are not as good as we imagined they would be. Change happens when we open our eyes to the brutality and unfairness and incongruity of life, and we begin to feel the pain of those we don't even know and never cared about.

Perhaps there is no greater evidence of God's love for us than that he allows us to become more like him. Satan's great lie in the Garden of Eden is God's great eternal promise. But Satan's game plan was not just at work with Adam and Eve. He continues to coax each of us every day. "You can change. I believe in you," the devil says. "Work hard enough, try often enough, plan extensively enough, and you can change yourself." Some well-meaning teachers promote the concept of God being embodied in each of us. But that is almost exactly what Satan promises. Because this philosophy feels warm, fuzzy, and friendly is precisely its danger. Satan didn't appear to be a slimy snake to Eve. He was attractive and friendly. He was on her side.

Change happens in us not because we will it,
but because we give up our will.

To truly experience the miracle of change in our lives, we must have the eyes to see the deception that pervades our modern philosophies and, in some cases, religions. The gospel of Christ is not "user friendly." The call to truly change—the gospel of repentance and sanctification—is not for the faint of heart or the weak of spirit.

God awards no points just because our pastor didn't preach sermons on the topic or we went along with what everyone in our Bible study believed. Christianity is not a democracy. We do not arrive at authentic personal faith by taking a vote. The excuses of Adam, "The woman gave me the fruit," sound similar to the excuses of the cripple at the pool in Bethesda. In neither case are the excuses even acknowledged. There is holy disdain for such human apologetics.

God's offer to change us is totally personal, good only if we deal directly and exclusively with him. It occurs in ways so mysterious that we may have a hard time articulating just what has occurred. It happens at levels so deep that to praise God for changing our motives, we have to admit just how sick our motivations were.

LAYERS OF DECEPTION

When God does change us, we can barely look back on what we were without total shame. I remember walking into a meeting one day after I had been praying fervently for God to change me any way he wanted. As I looked for a place to sit, I suddenly realized that I usually found a place near a man I'll call Greg. I was aware that he found me attractive and would compliment me on what I was wearing or support any comment I made during the meeting. It was a boost to my ego to sit near Greg.

God's offer to change us is totally personal,
good only if we deal directly and exclusively with him.

As I stood at the doorway, ready to go into the meeting, I was suddenly overwhelmed by the depth of my sin. I *wanted* Greg to be attracted to me. It wasn't that I planned to seduce Greg; I simply used him to stroke my ego. I didn't care what my flirtations did to him or if I was causing him to "lust in his heart." What I cared about was how it made me feel to be considered attractive and witty. Furthermore, I enjoyed having some control over Greg. In the meeting it gave me more power to know that Greg would always back me when I made a point.

I saw the empty seat next to Greg and hesitated. *Oh come on. You're making way too much of this,* I thought. *Just be a little more businesslike today. Don't flirt with him. It will be okay.* And then I knew that what seemed like a simple situation was a battle for my soul. *His feelings will be hurt if you don't sit by him,* I heard in my head. It sounded strangely like the voice of Satan in the garden. I uttered a quick prayer and sat between two women.

I was ashamed of myself, humiliated by the *bon vivant* attitude I had assumed in previous meetings. I was quiet that day, and someone asked me if I was feeling all right. I wanted to say, "No, I'm not feeling well at all. I am so sick I don't even know the depths of my self-deception. I love evil and have to struggle even to see what is righteous." I didn't say any of those things to the person who asked, but I confessed them to God. Whenever I think of that day and the insight I received, I am overwhelmed.

What happened within me that day might sound like a silly struggle to someone else. But to me it was life-altering. I had told God that I wanted to get well, and he had shown me how sick I really was. My motives were impure and twisted. And, worse, it was frighteningly easy for me to justify them.

When God begins to work within us, he often increases our sensitivity to evil. He shows us the sin within us and helps us see the deception of the world. What is surprising to me is how often I become aware of the depth of evil in seemingly good situations. The evil of pornography or murder or hatred is obvious. Even people who don't acknowledge what is holy can recognize what is unabashedly evil. As Christians, we have little to be proud of when we fight against such obvious foes. Satan must love it when we spend all of our energy on his red herrings.

*When God begins to work within us,
he often increases our sensitivity to evil.*

What Satan conceals so well—with our human consent—are the twisted motives and selfish agenda we begin to build on from the time we are old enough to make personal choices. One day I described to my husband a meeting I had attended for a nonprofit Christian organization. As I explained how the different parties were lobbying for their point of view (all in the name of God), he began to laugh. "This sounds like the meeting I had with a bunch of hard-nosed real estate developers today," he said. "The only difference is that we all knew we were out for our own deal. It sounds like the agenda was the same in your meeting, but no one acknowledged it." I had to admit he was right. Behind all the "God-talk" was selfishness, pure and simple.

To repent is to turn from evil to embrace the good that comes from God. It is often a remarkable experience because at that point we truly gain the knowledge of good and evil, seeing how bad evil is—in fact how bad we are—and how good God is, and how unlike him we are. Sanctification is the ongoing experience of turning toward God and away from evil. It is as if we declared our intentions through repentance and we live them out through sanctification. That we repent is a nuisance to Satan. That we take sanctification seriously is a serious threat to him.

HAVING EYES TO SEE

I know that God honors our desire to have our eyes opened. If we ask him to peel away the layers, he will help us see what we have never seen before. Sometimes he uses our circumstances to help reveal the stark reality that has hidden behind decorative disguises.

When I visited Guatemala, I went expecting to feel sorry for the people I met. Instead, I was surprised by the purity of joy and sorrow, the true happiness of people living with little but appreciating it more than those who have so much. When I returned to the United States I found myself revolted by situations that seemed normal only weeks before. Everyone had so much and was so unhappy. We seem to enjoy excess. I could hardly walk into my closet without running away in shame. I could have clothed a whole village with the variety of garments hanging there just for my enjoyment.

*I listened with ears that were cut by words like "I need"
spoken by people who have more than they could ever use.*

Weeks before I had been totally comfortable in my surroundings. I could have justified any aspect of my lifestyle. Now, having
lived with little, I saw how impoverished I was. I ached to think that
I lived in a home with empty rooms, while much of the world
crowded an entire family into an area smaller than my own family
room. I ate every meal with the knowledge that the very need of most
Americans to "diet" was an outrageous indictment of our squander-
ing of resources. And I listened with ears that were cut by words like
"I need" spoken by people who have more than they can ever use.

For days after I returned, I wandered my home and neighborhood like a visitor from another world, seeing for the first time what
was wrong with my lifestyle. But there was more. Somehow my sensitivities had been heightened in ways I could hardly explain. And
then someone gave me a copy of *Gracias!*, Henri Nouwen's journal
of his time in Latin America, and I discovered a passage that put
words to my feelings:

> In a world of poverty, the lines between darkness and light,
> good and evil, destructiveness and creativity, are much more dis-
> tinct than in a world of wealth.
>
> One of the temptations of the upper middle class is to cre-
> ate large gray areas between good and evil. Wealth takes away
> the sharp edges of our moral sensitivities and allows a comfort-
> able confusion about sin and virtue. The difference between rich
> and poor is not that the rich sin more than the poor, but that the
> rich find it easier to call sin a virtue. When the poor sin, they call
> it a sin; when they see holiness, they identify it as such. The intu-
> itive clarity is often absent from the wealthy, and that absence
> easily leads to the atrophy of the moral sense.[1]

That was what had happened to me! My moral sense had atro-
phied. I had enjoyed wallowing around in that gray area, comfortably
confused. And it was not that I had seen an ideal culture in Guatemala.
The poverty is devastating, the suffering of the children almost impossible to witness. And yet evil is evil there. In my comfortable home, the
word *evil* was hardly ever used. I began to see that my lifestyle, which
seemed so comfortable, was a constant seduction. I had walked away

for a week and returned a new person. But I was quickly sucked back into the comfort, the politeness, the "everyone does it" attitude that measures right and wrong against a flexible yardstick.

Thomas Merton calls this spiritual state "tepidity." He warns: "Tepidity, in which the soul is neither 'hot or cold'—neither frankly loves nor frankly hates—is a state in which one rejects God and rejects the will of God while maintaining an exterior pretense of loving him in order to keep out of trouble and save one's own supposed self-respect."[2]

MOVING TOWARD THE LIGHT

Few people use the word *evil* today. It sounds melodramatic, even hysterical. But in *People of the Lie*, Scott Peck doesn't hesitate to discuss the force that he had encountered as a psychologist; a force more complex than Freud or Jung or any psychiatrist had been able to cure. The force is evil, and in chilling description, he offers case studies in which seemingly normal people perpetuated twisted and perverse control over others.

Peck defines evil as "that force ... that seeks to kill life or liveliness." The opposite, he says, is described by the words of Jesus: "I have come that they may have life, and have it to the full" (John 10:10).

The life that Christ offers is not controlling or manipulative. The great mystery of free will is the ultimate expression of his love that neither controls nor manipulates us to come to him. We must take the steps in his direction. We must make the choices to walk toward the light.

We cannot delude ourselves with a false sense of goodness or righteousness because to do so means that we cannot see evil where it exists and name it for what it is. Recently I was talking to a group of friends about the horrors of Rwanda and Bosnia. In both cases people who had once lived peacefully as neighbors had turned on one another, perpetuating atrocities beyond comprehension. We were all shaking our heads at the madness, when one wise person said, "We have to admit that we could do it, too." We looked at him without understanding. "Until we see that we are capable of this kind of evil, we won't learn the lessons of it," he asserted.

The great mystery of free will is the ultimate expression of his love that neither controls nor manipulates us to come to him.

We debated his point for a while, at first all defending ourselves against the idea. Then slowly we began to admit our prejudices and frustrations. One person talked about the neighborhood fight over a new leash law and how the dog owners were pitted against those without pets. Another person remembered a twenty-year battle between her father and the man next door over who should mow the common area of grass between their properties. We laughed at some of the silly disagreements that had started major battles. Eventually, we began to see that within us is a great capacity for stubbornness and hatred that grows out of selfishness and a desire to control our lives and the lives of others. Although it is hard to imagine any disagreement growing into murder, we all admitted to times when a person who cut us off in traffic or a rude clerk had incited us to irrational behavior. Evil is in each and every one of us. It is hidden below a well-groomed exterior, a polite varnished veneer. Suddenly the wars in Rwanda and Bosnia took on a different look. There, but for the grace of God, were we.

LEARNING THE LESSONS OF EVIL

What good does it do to recognize evil? First, it gives us a different perspective on the world; a world in which such forces as evil exist is a world bigger and more complex than anything we can ever hope to control. Yes, there are powers beyond our human abilities and understandings, and we as humans have very little to do with them. No matter how good we are, no matter how careful, responsible, and resourceful, we are still subject to powers greater than we are.

*The more we are willing to expose our own evil,
the more capacity we have to change.*

But there is good news, too. Jesus says if we walk in the light, we have the companionship of those who are also seeking the light as well as the power of Christ to purify us (1 John 1:7). To recognize evil, especially in our own lives, is to expose it to light. And the more we are willing to expose our own evil, the more capacity we have to change. When we peel away the layers of our false innocence, feigned goodness, and noble intentions, we begin to get at the real foundations of our motives. We stop accusing others and making ourselves look good. We begin to see that even when others are doing wrong to us, our own instincts turn to pride and self-justification. We are truly beginning to live in the light when we stop spending so much time on the wrongs of others and begin to look at our own reactions to their infractions. We are moving closer to God when our own pain becomes less a source of focus than a way to see others' pain. We are growing in grace when we are less inclined to give answers to those who struggle and more inclined to put an arm around their shoulder and walk through the muck with them.

One of the greatest wrongs of modern day religion is the notion that those who follow Christ should think of themselves as superior to those who have not seen the light. But nothing in the teachings of Christ supports this perverse sense of pride. In fact, if anything, those of us who see Christ clearly are even more aware of our own short-comings, even more understanding of the grace that saves us. Following Christ does not put anyone on a pedestal. If anything, it knocks the pedestals out from beneath us and reminds us day in and day out that we are humanly capable of unimaginable evil. Yet Christians can also be a vessel of unimaginable good, not through force of will, but through surrender to God. It is a humbling proposition, one that never separates the saved from the sinner but instead lets the sinner see grace without judgment in a true servant of God.

QUESTIONS FOR REFLECTION

1. In what ways have you been tempted to listen to others instead of dealing directly with God? How can you change this tendency?
2. What are some of the philosophies of our day that minimize the difficulty of true change?
3. Look for signs of evil in your world. How are you tempted to justify thoughts and actions that you know are sinful?
4. How can you take the path of sanctification more seriously today?

Chapter Nine

ℒIVING AS A CHANGED PERSON

A lthough internal change is the miraculous work of God in our lives, a responsibility goes with this divine gift. To experience a change is an awesome epiphany, a miracle that often defies explanation. But to live as a changed person is quite another thing. It takes work to stay sober, remain open to others, continue to take responsibility for your actions, or exhibit patience instead of criticism. It takes discipline to hold on to the promise of change, to remain true to the calling that pulled you out of the ordinary and gave a glimpse of the divine. It is a mystery that must be made incarnate, or it is a gift that has no life beyond its birth.

Confronting the pain in life, listening to God's voice, giving up control and security, and acknowledging the evil within are all by-products of God's grace as he reaches into our lives and opens us to the infinite possibilities of living in the light. But our human tendencies are to avoid pain and seek control, to run from the truth about ourselves and design facades that make us look as though we are better than we are. We have to work at staying connected to the source of truth. We have to fight our delusions at every turn, or we will lapse into a state of temporal comfort at the cost of a shriveling soul.

God alone is able to change us. Our job is to be willing to be changed, to put ourselves in a position where God's ways can be our ways. It is our task to prepare our hearts and minds in order to see the hurts and needs and opportunities around us. Virginia Stem Owens puts it this way, "The enormous task is to keep your eyes open, your wick trimmed, your lamp filled, your powder dry.... There are no two ways about it. You've got your eyes open or you don't.... Seeking the kingdom is the essential integer."[1]

We have to fight our delusions at every turn, or we will lapse back into a state of temporal comfort at the cost of a shriveling soul.

How do we prepare ourselves for God's grace to work in our lives? I believe there are two types of preparations: spiritual and lifestyle. I make these distinctions because of the way I view these disciplines in my own life. To me, the spiritual disciplines include prayer, Scripture reading, worship, and confession. Lifestyle preparations—which I will cover in the next chapter—include simplicity, service, fasting, and witness. The lifestyle preparations unclutter my life so that I can hear and see God more clearly. The spiritual disciplines, however, are the things I do when I want to seek God's voice in a more deliberate way.

SPIRITUAL DISCIPLINES

There are many different spiritual disciplines, and some people find certain ones more helpful than others. The most common across various traditions are prayer, Bible study, worship, and confession.

Prayer

There was a simple plaque in my grandmother's house that I often read as a little girl. "Prayer changes things" it said, with vines swirling around the letters. As a child I often pondered its meaning. When I lost my favorite toy, I prayed to find it. When my dad was late coming home from work and my mother worried, I would sit in the window, watching for his car and praying. When I had a test at school, I would pray to do well. My interpretation was that when things weren't going my way, prayer could change them.

If I were to hang a plaque in my own home about prayer, it would read, "Prayer changes me." As an adult I know from personal experience that it is not so much how prayer affects others—and I believe it does—as how it affects me.

After I knew my baby had died and I was struggling to come to grips with the loss and the fear that I would lose my second baby as well, I had a hard time praying. It seemed strange to beg God to spare one child when the other had already died. Christ's words rang in my ears, "My God, my God, why hast thou forsaken me?" I know now that it is not unusual to feel forsaken by God when you have gone through difficulties. I also know that crying out to God in anger and anguish is one of the most honest prayers anyone can pray. For years I had said "nice prayers," trying to say the right words to reach God. Now I know that God prefers our honest prayers, even when they are cries of frustration, hurt, pain, or anger. He wants us to come clean with him.

It is not so much how prayer affects others — and I believe it does — as how it affects me.

When Tyler was finally born and I began to heal physically and emotionally, I still felt lost spiritually. At that point I feared that I would become bitter and closed off. So my simple request to God was, "Keep me open." I had no idea what it meant, but I can see now that it must have been music to God's ears. For the first time in my life, I had no preconceived notions of how God worked or how he would change things so they would go the way I had planned. I was simply laying my life out for him to work as he saw fit. I was, for the first time, willing to be prepared instead of in control.

That simple prayer was the beginning of the most significant changes in my life: the inner working of God on my heart to the point of realizing that whatever he wanted to do with me was what I wanted. As I look back to that point seven years ago, I am grateful that in my time of greatest despair, God heard me. It took weeks, even months, to begin to experience his presence, but as I did, it was in a totally new way. Even as I was feeling alone in my grief, God began to bring people into my life who became significant to me in my spiritual growth.

Prayer is one method of preparation. It is not just talking to God about me. It is also talking to God about other people. We usually call this intercessory prayer when we are asking God to help someone else. But there is another kind of prayer that I have also found to be important. It is telling God my honest feelings about someone I don't like — or love — as I should.

I once began to pray for a woman I worked with. Simply put, she drove me crazy. She was opinionated, self-centered, and legalistic. My motives for praying for her were all wrong; I wanted God to change her. Instead he began to work on me. Day after day I prayed for her to at least listen to others, and day after day I began to see what a poor listener *I* was. One day when she was spouting off, I asked her a question about her viewpoint. Suddenly, she softened, telling me about an event in her own life that had made her feel strongly about the issue. Then it made sense to me that she felt as she did. The more I prayed for the woman, the more I began to understand her. I saw that many of the traits that I disliked in her were in my personality as well. As I began to change, I found myself liking her more and more. God opened my eyes, not only to help see her needs, but also to see myself and what I needed to change. I grew not only to like this woman, but to truly love her in a way that I never would have thought humanly possible.

When I pray I admit that there is work to be done in my life.
Not only does prayer help me live as a changed person,
it helps me continue to be a changing person.

Prayer keeps me open in ways that I would never seek on my own. When I ask God to show me things in myself that need to change, when I ask him to point out people who need my help, I am relinquishing control and willingly handing over the reins of my life. When I pray I admit that there is work to be done in my life. Not only does prayer help me live as a changed person, it helps me continue to be a changing person.

Bible Study

I grew up in a church that emphasized Bible study above any other spiritual discipline. While I am grateful that I have a good knowledge of Scripture and have memorized many portions of the Bible, I view Bible study now as something that is a life-giving pastime rather than a badge to prove that I am "spiritual."

The words of the Bible are useful for "teaching, rebuking, correcting, and training in righteousness," according to 2 Timothy 3:16. At different points in our lives, the same words of Scripture may do any of these things. Sometimes verses are soothing to me, a reminder that God is with me even in the midst of chaos. Other times, they simply inspire me to keep on seeking him.

Some people use daily Bible study guides to help them work their way through the Bible; others simply read a chapter or two each day. I use a daily devotional book that references Scripture and often use that as the basis for further study in the Bible. I prefer to read my Bible in the morning, before the daily tasks crowd out any quiet moments. Some people prefer to read their Bible at night before going to bed. I see people reading Bibles on airplanes and on the subway. I have a very small Bible that fits easily into my purse. Carrying it with me provides more opportunity for reading it at odd moments during the day.

People I know who are truly the saints among us often have Bibles that are literally falling apart from reading.

Bible study becomes a habit not out of willpower, but because the more one studies the Bible, the more relevant it becomes. In the past I had had to work hard to stay awake through long passages; now I find myself reading long past the time I had allotted and seeking out favorite passages. Sometimes words that carried one meaning take on a new significance as daily events create a new context.

People I know who are truly the saints among us often have Bibles that are literally falling apart from reading. But I have also discovered that those of us who know how easy it is to live life as a sinner—those who have lived in darkness and light and understand the seduction of darkness—also have Bibles that are tattered from holding on to them, from clinging to the promises of God over the temptations of daily life.

The Bible is a powerful book that speaks to those who know God well and to those who hardly know him at all. A few years ago I was involved in a Bible study of women who expressed interest in knowing more about the Bible intellectually but did not necessarily want to approach the study spiritually. As the weeks went by and we studied the gospel of John, one by one the women began to express interest in the spiritual dimension of the Scriptures and particularly in the life of Jesus. As much as we tried to be objective in our study, even the most hardened souls softened as they studied the Bible for themselves. I was amazed as I saw the power of God's Word healing the pain in women's lives and bringing hope to those who had seemed at the end of their rope.

One woman who was very well educated and well read said, "This book is more interesting than anything I have ever read." For those of us who have grown up with the Bible, it is sometimes easy to underestimate its power. But the Bible is truly the *living* Word of God as it becomes part of our life and a source of daily light.

Worship

Worship is a word that has lost much of its value in today's world. We worship our bodies, our cars, and our possessions and find that all of them deteriorate or lose their luster over time. To worship something truly greater than our human understanding is foreign to today's way of thinking. Unlike ancient societies, our gods are not mysterious or powerful; they can be bought with a credit card and paid for over time.

To worship God truly is to acknowledge that he is all-powerful, all-knowing, and all-present. It is to admit that to be human is to have an overblown sense of importance. But worship of God does not mean denigration of self. It means, instead, to be so caught up in adoration of God that self is simply forgotten.

We have built churches to remind us of the One who is greater than the mundane world in which we spend our lives. In a sense, worship is when we stand on tiptoes with arms extended, trying to hug our heavenly Father.

But for those of us who are blessed to live in or near natural beauty, worship is often best accomplished in nature, where we can look at God's handiwork and rejoice that he has shared it with us. Worship reminds us that the world is not really ours and that we are travelers who should be good stewards of the surroundings. "Don't let artificial light and city streets keep you from noticing sunsets and sunrises, from experiencing the spring of new life and the harvest of fall," says M. Basil Pennington in *A Place Apart.* "If you don't have a farm, at least have a window box or a few pots of earth."

To worship God is to remind ourselves of the point at which we are aiming: the goal of our changing and becoming new. Worship lifts us out of the muck of daily existence with all of its frustrations and temptations and sets us temporarily on a plateau. When we go back to reality, we can hum the "Hallelujah Chorus" and be transported momentarily to the place where our burdens are light and our soul lifts the rest of our body heavenward.

Confession

For those who grew up in the Catholic church, confession was part of a formal ritual. For Protestants, confession is something that is talked about often but done less readily. In fact, "don't ask, don't tell" might better describe the way many of us view the treatment of sins in the church. Yet we lose out on a sacred principle when we fail to confess our sins to one another. Says Richard Foster in *Celebration of Discipline*, "The discipline of confession brings an end to pretense. God is calling into being a church that can openly confess its frail humanity and know the forgiving and empowering graces of Christ. Honesty leads to confession, and confession leads to change."

Confession takes away all pretense and shows us who we really are while reminding us of what we can become.

To confess our wrong intentions, improper actions, and evil ways is to lose our pride and expose our inner self to the cleansing power of the Light. It is to see sin for what it is and to make no excuses for our willingness to take part in it. Confession embarrasses, exposes, and humiliates the human parts of us while cleansing and irrigating our soul. Confession helps clean the rot away so that we can grow again. Confession takes away all pretense and shows us who we really are while reminding us of what we can become.

Some things should be confessed to the person we have wronged, some to a friend or group of trusted friends who can keep us from falling back into our bad habits; and some to a larger body in an appropriate setting. All of these sins and more should be confessed to God. In fact, I often ask God to show me what I need to confess since I am aware that my ability to hide sin even from myself is well developed.

To continue to become new we have to continue to give up what is old. As we walk with God we begin to see more things within that are exposed by the light. Once we see them we have no choice but to confess them and turn away. To hold on to them after that would be to harden our soul. Confession cracks through the hard shell of pride and self-deceit and allows us to change even more.

KEEPING PERSPECTIVE

The spiritual disciplines should never be an end in themselves. If we go about them as legalistic imperatives, we make a religion of them. The sad truth is that there are many people who have made the disciplines their religion and are further from being changed people than those who live carefree lives.

The Pharisees loved disciplines and rules. They even used them against Jesus and his followers. Annie Dillard says it well: "Experience has taught the race that if knowledge of God is the end, then these habits of life are not the means but the condition in which the means operates. You do not have to do these things; not at all. God does not, I regret to report, give a hoot. You do not have to do these things—unless you want to know God. They work on you, not him."[2]

Over the centuries and throughout various religious traditions, people who have seriously sought God have developed certain disciplines that have enabled them to hear God's voice more clearly and more readily follow his call. Some traditions have gone to the extreme of human deprivation and even self-flagellation. Some have raised up certain disciplines as paths toward God and then, over the years, begun to worship the disciplines themselves. Some individuals feel a need to lead a monastic life in order to stay connected to God; others seem most connected in the hustle and bustle of daily life.

Whatever the case, disciplines are human devices to help us stay connected to that which we have a hard time seeing or hearing in the midst of the ordinary. For me, leading a spiritually disciplined life means that my human cravings diminish and I actually begin to hunger for God.

Perhaps it is helpful to think of these activities as preparations rather than disciplines. Anyone who enjoys the exhilaration of speeding down a ski run knows that the sense of joy and freedom is preceded by time to adjust the bindings on the skis, buy lift tickets, stand in line, and ride the lift up the mountain. So, too, our spiritual mountaintop experiences are made possible not only by God's grace, but also by our desire to stay prepared.

THE IMPORTANCE OF PERSEVERANCE

There are times in our lives when we seem to experience spiritual growth spurts, when God seems near to us, even in the midst of difficulties. And there are other times when we struggle to remember what God's voice sounds like, when the glare of the streetlights seems more illuminating than the promise of divine light. During those times of doubt and longing, our spiritual disciplines keep us on track. And when we connect again with God, we often discover that the Bible reading that seemed uninspiring, or the prayers that felt unanswered, become meaningful in hindsight.

Ask any sailor what he or she dreads the most, and you'll rarely hear a hurricane or rough seas. Instead, the universal frustration of every sailor is to be "in irons"—without enough wind to move in any direction. It is downright dangerous if you have no engine and are near shore or rocks. Sometimes I feel as if my spiritual life is "in irons." I must stay focused even without the obvious movement of the wind.

A few years ago I heard a heartbreaking news story. The Marines had been on maneuvers in the desert, far away from civilization. When they finished their war games, they pulled out, taking all of their equipment with them. Although they thought that everyone was accounted for, they overlooked one of the young men.

> *I must stay focused even without
> the obvious movement of the wind.*

Left behind in the desert without rations or equipment, he began to walk toward what he thought was civilization. The man walked more than ten miles in searing heat and without water before he fell down exhausted and gave up. They found his body there, ironically, less than a mile from a major highway where he would have certainly found help. I always wondered if he would have been able to walk just one more mile if he had known.

This tragic true story reminds me of the scene in *African Queen* where Humphrey Bogart and Katherine Hepburn have survived alligators, rapids, savages, and poachers in their struggle down a jungle river in an effort to reach Lake Victoria. After all they have gone through, their boat becomes stuck in a marsh full of leeches. Bogart jumps out of the boat and pushes it as long as he can under the scorching sun. Then he gets back in the boat, and Hepburn pulls the leeches from him so he can start the process over again. Finally they both collapse in the bottom of the boat, certain they are going to die despite their efforts. As the camera pans back on them in the boat, the viewer sees that the marsh lasts only a few more yards before it opens into the sweeping waters of Lake Victoria. But for all Bogart and Hepburn know, they have miles to go before reaching their goal. They are certain they are going to perish. They don't have the big picture. All they see are weeds and leeches.

Sometimes our spiritual lives seem like they are mired in the marshes, far from the open waters. We struggle and seek answers that don't seem to come. We ask, "How much longer?" and hear only the echo of our words in response. We wonder if we will ever see change in ourselves, in our loved ones, or in a situation that seems hopeless.

In those days of despair, the disciplines become important. Through simple obedience we find the strength to go on. And later, when we have come to the open waters, we can look back on the times of despair and realize that through them we have grown. Because of them we are able to take the next step in becoming all we are meant to be.

The disciplines themselves don't change us. But our willingness to obey does.

QUESTIONS FOR REFLECTION

1. Have you ever prayed for someone you dislike? Try praying for an "enemy" today and see what happens.
2. Are you being totally honest with God when you pray? Are you angry, frustrated, or disillusioned? Have you told him how you feel?
3. What "gods" do you worship? Fashion? Cars? Your job?
4. How can you truly worship God today?
5. Who do you know well enough to confess your problems to?
6. How can you be more honest with God as you confess your sins?
7. Is your spiritual life stalled? What will you do today to change?

Chapter Ten

TRAVELING LIGHT

W hen Tom and I were first married, we had a small car, a few clothes, some secondhand dishes, and a few pieces of furniture. We vowed never to buy anything that wouldn't fit into our hatchback so that we could pack up and take off if the spirit moved. It was probably fanciful thinking even then, but after seventeen years of marriage we have accumulated enough stuff that the idea of moving anywhere is daunting.

Recently we had central air conditioning added to our old house, and in displacing the piles in the attic for the workers to add ducts, we were horrified by the number of boxes we were simply storing, full of possessions. After placing half a dozen boxes on our front porch for the Salvation Army, we still had piles left. We realized we had become pack rats, and we vowed to do something about our accumulation.

LIFESTYLE DISCIPLINES

Most of us lead cluttered lives. Besides the clutter of possessions, we fill our lives with diversions, messy relationships, and meaningless busyness. Sometimes it seems that we spend our lives sorting and storing, unscrambling and explaining. There is little joy in simple pleasures. We rarely take the time to appreciate even the good things that happen. And there is little time left for service to others or to witness to the greatness of God. We are more likely to spend our hours searching for accessories or comparing notes with friends on the latest style or the newest gadget.

Perhaps one of the reasons that we have such a hard time following God in today's world is that God has to shout to be heard over the din of our lives. And yet God rarely shouts; more often he whispers, and our ears have to be sensitive to hear his words.

Perhaps one of the reasons that we have such a hard time following God in today's world is that God has to shout to be heard over the din of our lives.

To open my ears to God's whispers, I have learned the importance of practicing what I call "lifestyle disciplines": simplicity, service, fellowship, and witness. While spiritual disciplines help me focus on my relationship with God, lifestyle disciplines help me focus on my relationship with my fellow human beings and with my world.

Simplicity

The clutter and clamor of our world is one of the most destructive forces in our spiritual lives. To move away from the seduction of accumulations and busyness takes discipline. It takes an effort to resist the constant messages that tell us to consume, the regular appeals for our time, and the seduction of tastes, smells, and sounds that dull our sensitivities. It does not take living the life of an ascetic to stay tuned in to God, but it does take a move toward simplicity to keep us able to be open and responsive to God.

To move away from the seduction of accumulations and busyness takes discipline.

My friend, Colleen "Coke" Townsend Evans, is one of the most beautifully spiritual people I know. I have never felt her disapproval, yet I have always learned from her. She has never criticized me, but whenever I am with her, I see something that I want to emulate. One of Coke's spiritual principles is that of traveling light. In fact, she often speaks on this topic at retreats. She speaks about keeping things simple so that at a moment's notice she can be used by God. And she lives the life she speaks about. She is slim and trim, not through dieting, but through eating simply and at times skipping meals to fast and pray. She never talks about such things unless she is asked, but I have noticed that she is very grateful for the food she does eat.

She uses public transportation whenever she can; dresses beautifully but simply, often in clothes found in secondhand shops; and speaks little but listens well, often dropping notes of encouragement to friends who are struggling. There is a peace and wisdom about Coke that exudes from her and is evident to anyone who comes in contact with her. She is one of the most open people I know, willing to listen to God and not be set in her ways.

When I think of how I want to live and how I can best be open and responsive to God, I know that uncluttering my life is one of the principles I must follow. But it is not enough to want to live simply; it takes a determined effort to choose a path of less, not more. It takes discipline to resist the advertising messages that assault me and lead me to believe that my clothes need updating, my hair could use accessorizing, and the jewelry I have is already out of style.

I find myself walking through a shopping mall wondering what I "need," involved in the dangerous habit of recreational shopping. And yet one of my recent complaints was that I didn't have enough storage space for my clothes and that my shoes had outgrown my shoe rack. Overconsumption is very much like overeating. Once you start bingeing it becomes a habit. You are hungry all of the time, even after you should be full.

In choosing to simplify my life, I began by giving away the things I didn't use regularly. This was more difficult than I had thought. I came across clothes I'd forgotten and reasoned that I might wear them now. I hesitated to give away favorites and hoped that the weight I planned to lose would mean that I could fit back into the skirts that had gone unworn since my last pregnancy. The process was far more difficult than I had imagined it would be, showing me further the depths of my attachments to things.

The discipline of simplicity revealed a whole new level of needed change in my life.

꿏   ꙮ

Next, I was determined to shop infrequently and only when I truly needed something. I tried to buy regular items like pantyhose in bulk and even found a mail order catalog that offered my brand at a reduced price. I made a game of seeing how long I could go without entering a shopping mall. At lunchtime I tried to go for walks (passing stores) and find exhibits or other free destinations. I found a church that was open at noon and went in to pray about my compulsions that seemed to have no end.

I also decided to cut back on my eating and to learn to see food as a fuel for my body, not as a reward or substitute or stress reducer. I began to choose water instead of soft drinks and tried to increase my fiber through fruits and vegetables and decrease non-nutritious junk foods and fats. I began to ask myself why I was eating and was surprised at how often I put things in my mouth for reasons other than hunger.

The discipline of simplicity revealed a whole new level of needed change in my life. I began to see all of the things that were crutches for me. I began to recognize how often I shopped or ate instead of dealing with more basic issues in my life. On a whole new level I began to see how sick I really was. And as I have continued to take further steps to simplify my life, I have been able to see more clearly how God wants to work through me.

Service

In the next chapter we will talk extensively about having a personal ministry to others. But as a discipline, service means taking on an attitude that is servant-like in all that we do. Often pride is a motivator for what we do. Pride is a great temptation in today's world. We are rewarded for accomplishments and praised, even in the church, for being important and powerful. Being willing to serve others gets us little credit.

Quiet, even anonymous service is a discipline that has a very deep effect on us if we practice it regularly. Trying to do good every day, without acknowledgment or reward, is a discipline that takes us out of ourselves and begins to put to work the changes that have happened within. Serving others is a sacrament that keeps us connected to God in a paradoxical way. How is it that by doing the most lowly work we connect to the Almighty? Perhaps it is because the Lord says, "... whatever you did for one of the least of these brothers of mine, you did for me" (Matt. 25:40).

Quiet, even anonymous service is a discipline that has a very deep effect on us if we practice it regularly.

But even in society, choosing to serve has a certain significance. At some point in our lives, we all end up doing things that are beneath our dignity. Parenthood is full of such moments, from diaper changings to serving meal after meal to hungry masses of friends. But actually choosing to take on the lowest tasks at work or on a church committee sets a person apart, especially if he or she does that task with commitment and dignity.

When my father was suffering through his last days, he was often attended by a nurse who dealt with his needs efficiently and tenderly. She was exceptional in her skills but also willing to do tasks usually left for the orderlies if it made my father more comfortable. One day she told me that she had worked in an intensive care unit and had qualifications that enabled her to work for far more pay in a more prestigious job. But she chose to work in a convalescent home, aiding dying and chronically ill patients. She did it partially so that she had more time at home with her child but also because she said she sensed that she received something back by helping others in a way that was not so much a matter of skill but of attitude. She would never go back to the kind of job she'd had before, she told me. She had chosen to serve and in doing so she had been changed.

Fellowship

We usually think of fellowship as a time when we come together with people of similar belief to worship God. But fellowship is any time when two or more people are gathered in God's name. It could be over lunch or tennis, in serving together or simply enjoying each other's company.

With my close Christian friends I can be totally open and vulnerable, and they understand that the context in which I confess is not false humility but true struggle. They also know that when I celebrate progress, I am praising God's grace, not my own self-discipline. When I struggle, they support me. When I need reminders of God's presence, they supply the words. When I am angry with God, they keep me from walking away from him.

*Fellowship is any time when two or more people
are gathered in God's name.*

Because we are all different yet united in our faith, we can help one another see things that individually we might miss. We can encourage one another and call each other to accountability. We can help solve each other's problems and help each other avoid difficulties. We can point the way to God in a diverse yet united chorus.

Thomas Kelly puts it this way in his book *A Testament of Devotion*:

> Two people, three people, ten people may be in living touch with another through Him who underlies their separate lives. This is an astounding experience, which I can only describe but cannot explain in the language of science. But in a vivid experience of divine Fellowship it is there. We know that these souls are with us, lifting their lives and ours continuously to God and opening themselves, with us, in steady and humble obedience to Him. It is as if the boundaries of our self were enlarged, as if we were within them and as if they were within us. Their strength, given to them by God, becomes our strength, and our joy, given to us by God, becomes their joy.[1]

Witness

To some people witness means an evangelization process of articulating their beliefs to those who don't believe. To me, witness is far broader than handing a tract to someone or preaching on a corner. Witness is living in such a way that God's love actually shines through, that Christ's sense of priorities are clearly seen in our priorities. Mother Teresa's life is a witness. Her actions make no sense in the context of what the world values, and yet even the most pagan person can see that she lives a life of faith that is transcendent yet deeply rooted in daily struggles to alleviate suffering.

"You can never give another person that which you have found, but you can make him homesick for what you have," says Oswald Chambers in *My Utmost for His Highest*. Our task, then, is not to give quick answers to the needy but to make them homesick for what they know they need. Faith is not a quick fix or an easy solution. But it is a journey that is exciting and fulfilling, something that others should want to join us on, not run when they see us coming. It is not so much that we should make it look easy. It is rather that our sense of focus and centering should stand out in a world where people are searching for something or Someone to believe in.

Witness is a discipline, but it is also a lifestyle. Witness means not only to speak of God, but also to live like we are his. Witness is more pervasive than a social cause, a political agenda, or a personal hobby. It is becoming a person who reflects back to the Creator that which he or she was created to be. As Oswald Chambers writes, witnessing is "Where no one thinks of noticing you, all that is noticed is that the power of God comes through you all the time."[2]

Witness is a discipline, but it is also a lifestyle.

How do we truly witness to God's presence in all that we do? Part of the mystery of this discipline is that by trying not to be noticed ourselves, we bring notice to God. By trying not to preach, but by living more like the hands and feet of God on earth, we preach with more than words. By proclaiming that God is all-important, we truly stand out in a crowd of people trying to draw attention to themselves.

And witness is words, too. We speak naturally of that which we love. Even if it sounds foreign in the objective world, we must speak of spiritual things within the context of daily life. We must not be afraid to say God's name in a world that mostly takes it in vain. We don't need to hide the importance of the other disciplines any more than we would think of hiding that we jog every day to stay in shape physically.

By proclaiming that God is all important, we truly stand out in a crowd of people trying to draw attention to themselves.

Witness is the most encompassing of all the disciplines, incorporating all of the others under its pervasive umbrella. It is both a conscious and unconscious expression of the changes within us. And the visible changes in us are ways in which others see that God is at work in the world and in our lives, doing a new thing.

Simplicity. Service. Fellowship. Witness. These four "lifestyle disciplines" help us to put into concrete action what we have learned through the spiritual disciplines of prayer, Scripture reading, worship, and confession. Through us, the Spirit bubbles into life, changing us, others, and the world. Because we are changed, we are then able to change the world. And suddenly, change begins to happen, not only *in* us, but also *because* of us. And that is the greatest miracle of all.

QUESTIONS FOR REFLECTION

1. In what ways has your life become cluttered? How can you simplify your possessions? Your relationships? Your consumption?
2. What can you do for someone else today that no one will ever know about?
3. Do you have a group of friends who believe as you do and encourage you to grow? If not, consider joining—or starting—a Bible study group.
4. How do people know that you are a believer from the way you live your life? How does your faith make a difference in the way you act toward others?

Part Three

WHEN CHANGE HAPPENS BECAUSE OF US

Chapter Eleven

$\mathscr{G}$IVING BACK

To change within is a miraculous, personal experience. It is often difficult to explain to others and is only understood on a level that defies human logic. We are to embody that change through personal discipline, and then we need to celebrate that change by giving something back. We are to thank God for every day we are sober, every time we feel the pain of someone we would have ignored before, every moment when a harsh word rises up and we suppress it instead of spewing it at someone else. These are miracles, pure and simple. They are no less awesome than making the blind to see or the deaf to hear. They represent a change of course, a divine intervention in human stubbornness.

Besides celebrating, we are also to act on our new insight. We are supposed to be a new person inside and out. Once we have seen the light, we are to use it to illuminate our path. Said Paul in Ephesians 5:8–10: "For you were once in darkness, but now you are light in the Lord. Live as children of light (for the fruit of the light consists in all goodness, righteousness and truth) and find out what pleases the Lord."

> *Once we have seen the light,*
> *we are to use it to illuminate our path.*

The words in James are even more direct: "Anyone, then, who knows the good he ought to do and doesn't do it, sins" (James 4:17). What an awesome challenge to those of us who have learned not to get involved.

It doesn't take more than a quick reading of the morning paper or a review of the day's news to know that the world is in trouble. The problems of crime, poverty, violence, and moral indifference plague our society. It seems as though the issues are too great to deal with, and yet we have all heard stories about one person whose life has made a difference. Each of us is called to change what we can, whether we feel qualified or not.

INDIVIDUALS CAN MAKE A DIFFERENCE

Linda Beams never set out to change the world. In fact, the somewhat shy mother from Texas would have been one of the most unlikely candidates to take on someone as loud and confident as Geraldo Rivera. But take him on she did in a match that can only be compared to David versus Goliath.

It all started when Linda realized her adolescent son was coming home from school, turning on the television, and being greeted by the Geraldo show and themes like "parents who killed their children" or topics of sexual perversion. She figured her son wasn't that unusual—lots of kids come home from school and turn on the television around 4:00 P.M. And she also realized that kids who came home to an empty house or a baby-sitter might actually watch the show that she made sure her own son clicked right past.

So she wrote a polite letter to her local television station requesting that the show be moved to a more appropriate time when the likelihood of children watching without supervision was minimal. When she didn't get a response, she decided that maybe advertisers didn't realize what was actually on the show. So she taped several episodes, sent them to the sponsors, and once again suggested that the material on the shows did little to help the sponsors or children who might be watching. Several sponsors withdrew their support of the show altogether.

But the station thought that Beams was attempting to censor the show, despite her continued assertion that she simply wanted it moved to a more appropriate time slot. The local station manager dug in his heels and fought Linda in a public campaign. Letters began to flood the station and the show from parents who shared Linda's concern. Geraldo then announced that he had decided to move away from some of the more sensational topics and return to more investigative reporting. Many saw this as an attempt to slow his loss of sponsors.

Finally, after two years, Linda's local station dropped the show altogether, admitting that viewer complaints had risen considerably.

A few years later, most local stations began placing talk shows with more sensitive topics in time slots during school hours. Now the slots from 4:00 P.M. until the news are dominated by children's shows and some of the "cleaner" talk shows. Linda's hometown cause became a national campaign and has changed both the nature of some shows and the way sponsors support them.

If anyone had told Linda Beams that she could change the way all local stations select programming, she would have laughed. She was just a homemaker from Fort Worth. But today Linda knows that if God wants Christians to make changes in their world, he will give them the wisdom and the opportunity to take on giants—and win.

If God wants Christians to make changes in their world, he will give them the wisdom and the opportunity to take on giants—and win.

Valerie Bell was another homemaker who had quit working outside her home in order to spend more time with her children. But once she was home she discovered that the entire neighborhood seemed to flock to her house, and other mothers routinely let their children hang out while they ran errands.

Valerie was feeling a bit resentful of this intrusion when one night she had a dream. In it she was presented with a brand-new baby. She was thrilled at the prospect of another child. But when she looked at its face, it wasn't one of her own children but one of the kids from the neighborhood who was especially annoying. When Valerie awakened, she knew that God was reminding her that she had a responsibility to her neighborhood children, too.

So Valerie decided to actually invite the kids to her home, make an attempt to get to know each of them, and to pray for them. She invited them to eat dinner with the family, provided soft drinks during the day, and let her home become the official hangout for the neighborhood. She became what she calls a "Kool-Aid Mom."

Soon she discovered that she was able to change the lives of many of the children who were lonely or dealing with difficult situations at home. And the parents loved that Valerie was so giving. They didn't even mind that she taught the kids Bible stories and shared her faith with them.

Valerie has seen several of the neighborhood children come to faith in Christ through her efforts. She knows that ministering to these children was what she was called to do in her neighborhood. In her book, *Reaching Out to Lonely Kids*, she encourages other parents to reach out to the kids in their neighborhoods, too.

PERSONAL MINISTRIES

When we hear about women like Linda or Valerie and think that they had something special that motivated them, we think it sounds so easy. But having met both of these women, I recognize that each faced a moment when it would have been easier simply to make a rule or turn away than it was to step out in faith on a course that wasn't easy or sure. Wouldn't it have been easier for Linda just to deal with her own son and then simply complain to a friend about the terrible shows on television? Couldn't Valerie have just taken her own kids to the park to get away from the neighborhood throngs? Don't we all— every day—solve our own problems without thinking about how we could make the world a little better for someone else?

Dr. Roberta Hestenes, president of Eastern College, spoke recently to a conference on the subject of reconciliation. She said that one of the reasons we fail to reconcile with each other in our society is that we have taken up a modern day mantra: "It's not my fault. It's not my responsibility." As long as we repeat these two phrases often enough, we will never have to grow ourselves or reach out to help others.

We have raised the cause of individualism to a high art. In some parts of the country people live side by side and hardly know each other. People go about their lives without human contact except at a cash register. And all the time we read the newspapers and shake our heads about the mess our society is in. As human beings, we have a responsibility to act. As Christians, we have the power to make a difference.

God has put you where you are for a reason and given you the abilities needed to make a difference.

We're all busy. We rush around from the time we wake up until the time we go to bed, with little time for our own families. But I believe that if we ask God to help us, he will show us where our personal ministry should be. It doesn't have to be a big deal. Maybe it's just visiting a nursing home you pass as you drive home from work. Maybe it's delivering a meal to a widower in your neighborhood or dropping a note of encouragement to a friend. Maybe it's a ministry to someone in your own family. Whatever it is, God has put you where you are for a reason and given you the abilities needed to make a difference.

HOW TO MAKE A DIFFERENCE

As Christians we are called to act on every opportunity to do good. So where do we begin? After interviewing many ordinary people who have made a difference in the world, I have learned these basics of helping: ask God to show you the needs he wants you to meet, be willing to act, help just one person at a time, don't look for personal glory, and minister to those who are "close to home."

Ask God to Show You the Needs He Wants You to Meet

One of the characteristics I have noticed about the people I admire most is that they seem to have a special instinct for noticing those in need. It is a rare gift to take the time and have the inclination to look for the needs in those around you. When I asked my friend Mary why she had dropped me a note that I received on an especially difficult day she said, "I just ask God to bring to mind people in need, and that day I thought of you."

One of the characteristics I have noticed about the people I admire most is that they seem to have a special instinct for noticing those in need.

Now I try to pray and ask God to show me each day the "good I ought to do." It's just too easy to be blind to the needs around me; not to ask one more question that will reveal a problem or loneliness. When I do this consistently, I have learned that I feel as if my senses are heightened. I almost feel as though I am on a treasure hunt throughout the day, looking for someone I can help.

One day I was reminded of a friend who struggles with self-esteem and dropped her a note. A few weeks later she saw me in a store and threw her arms around me. "How did you know I was desperate the day your note arrived?" she asked. I had a great sense of satisfaction knowing that my friend Mary had inspired me to help someone else. Another time I listened, really listened, to a neighbor who called to pass along some information. When I asked a simple follow-up question, she began to cry, revealing pain she had been hiding for years.

In neither case was I being particularly sensitive, but I was willing to be used by the spirit of God, and he seemed to use me to do his good work. I believe it is somewhat dangerous to throw ourselves in to good works without the power of the Holy Spirit in it. It is too easy to become overburdened, codependent, or to feel like a martyr. It is also tempting to feel proud of our accomplishments without fully participating in the joy of unselfish ministry to others. Just as prayer changes me, so does ministry. Whatever I have been able to do for someone else has often been far more significant to me as I have reaped the spiritual blessings from simply being obedient. The rewards are not the same when I do something out of a sense of duty.

Be Willing to Act

My husband was attending a party once when a woman's hair caught on fire. He was shocked to see everyone just standing and watching for a moment. Although he wasn't closest to her, he was the first to have the sense and ability to act. Grabbing her, he put out the flames with his own shirt. He insisted he wasn't a hero, just someone who knew that every second counts in an emergency.

When we see a problem or someone struggling, we are often hesitant to get involved for good reasons. Maybe we don't understand the situation. Maybe we don't have time. Maybe we fear we'll get hurt. Maybe we think that if we start to help someone, we'll never get away. These are all valid human reasons. But as Christians we really don't have a choice. It is our responsibility, even when it isn't our fault.

My father was one of the greatest Good Samaritans I have ever known. As a child I was sometimes embarrassed that my father could hardly go through a store without helping someone. It seemed to me that at times he was sticking his nose into other people's business. But as I grew up, I saw how years of looking out for others had trained my father to watch for anyone who was about to drop a bag of groceries or who needed a hand with a door. Daddy was usually the first on the scene with a helping hand because he was actually looking for people to help.

My father was one of those people who would have given someone the shirt off his own back—and been delighted that he could help. He once told me, "It is such a blessing to be able to help other people. Never forget how fortunate you are when you are able to give to someone else." At his funeral, person after person came up to me and told me a story of my father loaning money or helping somone move or giving an employee a day off to take care of personal problems. I was surprised by the number of people I didn't know, but they knew and remembered my father. And I was also amazed at the number of things he had done for other people that I had never heard about. My father was one of the happiest people I have ever known. I am convinced that much of his joy came from seeing someone in need and acting on his impulses.

Help Just One Person at a Time

Bob Pierce, founder of World Vision, never envisioned a global ministry operating in more than ninety countries. He just wanted to help one Korean orphan. And then he helped another and another.

What a change we can make if we invest ourselves in individuals.

Anne Ortlund never planned to have a discipling ministry. She just began a Bible study in her home for three women after taking seriously the biblical imperative to "disciple one another." Those women went on to teach others, and Anne started another group of five women. Twenty years later, more than six hundred women who were first-, second-, or third-generation disciples of Anne were invited to a party to celebrate her life. Her step-by-step obedience had translated into a world-changing ministry.

We can only change our world one person at a time. But what a change we can make if we invest ourselves in individuals. Too often we think that we can only have an impact if we appear on a television show or on a speaking platform. But lives are most often changed by individuals who take an interest and invest themselves in others.

Says Valerie Bell, "Sometimes we women think that we need to have big ministries to make a difference. But I'm convinced that God wants us to fill the small spaces in our world. That's how he can use us to be influential."

Don't Look for Personal Glory

Any one of us can help a neighbor or listen to a lonely friend. But when we do it with a belief that God is in it, we become someone more than who we are. We become a conduit of God's mercy and grace, and I believe the recipient of our help can feel that difference. There is no shame in accepting that type of help. It does not feel like a handout or an act of charity. We don't feel sorry for the person or expect their thanks. There is a certain mystery in the act because it is sacramental in nature. We are doing to "the least of these" and thereby doing unto God.

When we free ourselves and the recipient from human expectations, we stop the cynical questions ("Why is she doing this for me? What will she want in return?") as well as our own natural impulses ("He better be grateful for this. I've gone to a lot of trouble. I hope she appreciates it.") Our bargain is not between us and the person we serve. Our only deal is with God. We are simply being obedient. The reaction of the person we help has no bearing on what we do. Even if we are met with ungratefulness or rejection, we have done what we are supposed to do and can be assured that God will use our obedience.

If we do something like Linda Beams did, we could be tempted to become a crusader after the one victory, always searching for others. But once Linda had accomplished what she set out to do, she simply credited God and went back to being a mom. Some people urged her to start an organization or a newsletter. But Linda felt strongly that God had not asked her to start an enterprise. He had only called her to act on the one incident that affected her family. She was happy to go back and wait for him to show her the next way to minister.

Even if we are met with ungratefulness or rejection,
we have done what we are supposed to do
and can be assured that God will use our obedience.

Some people have started organizations out of their simple acts of obedience. If that is what God calls them to do, I believe he will help the ministry prosper. But I also know that much can be done without a name or a charter or a newsletter. In fact, simple acts done in God's name can often change hearts more than mailings or telethons or crusades.

Giving the glory to God has become one of those phrases we have heard so many times that it starts to lose meaning. But when we minister, doing it in God's name is most important.

Minister to Those Who Are "Close to Home"

When we think of ministry, the temptation is to think of far-off lands and people who are different than we are. But often I think God asks us to look at those closest to us and to be willing to invest in their lives first. How unglamorous to work in our own neighborhood, yet what a difference we could make.

I heard about a retired couple who live in a condominium with many elderly neighbors. When the couple received a bread maker for Christmas, they decided to make a loaf of bread each day and deliver it to a different resident. Their daily gift probably means more than they will ever know to the people in their building.

I know another woman who prays for her neighbors, house by house, each day. Once at a neighborhood party she met a man she had never seen, but when he told her where he lived, she blurted out, "Oh, I was just praying for you last Tuesday." Her comment led to a discussion about faith. A week later the man appeared at her door with a smile on his face and a Bible in his hand. "I started reading this again because of you," he said. "Thank you."

If you've ever been asked to collect for the Heart Association or for the American Cancer Society, you've probably groaned about it. But going door to door for a good cause is a great way to learn a little about the people who live near you. What about initiating a neighborhood potluck or starting a prayer group at your school for parents to gather and pray for the teachers and the school? When we started an early morning prayer group at our school, we received notes of thanks from several teachers who appreciated that we were supporting them. What about starting a backyard Bible school next summer? Lots of kids need a place to go while they are out of school, and many parents are grateful for the opportunity to do without a baby-sitter.

You *can* change your world if you trust God and look around you. It doesn't have to take a great deal of time. And the rewards are well worth the investment. While you are changing your world, you will probably find that you have changed, too.

QUESTIONS FOR REFLECTION

1. Have you asked God to show you ways that you are uniquely able to help others?
2. Think about the people on your block or in your neighborhood. How could you help just one person this week?
3. What frustrates you? Is there something in your school, church, or community that needs changing? What can you do to help make it better?
4. Are you willing to write one note a week to encourage, voice an opinion, or suggest a way to change the world?

Chapter Twelve

THE LEGACY OF CHANGE

I was making dinner in the kitchen when I heard yelling from the boys' bedrooms. "I can't believe you broke my model," Chase cried angrily.

"I'm sorry, Chase, it was an accident," responded Tyler, his six-year-old voice sounding younger in his despair. "I'm really, really sorry."

I was about to intervene when I heard Chase's voice again and froze in my tracks. "Well, sorry isn't good enough," he said with a scathing tone. "You should have been paying attention."

I shuddered as I realized I had said those very words to him a few days before. And that tone of voice was cold and harsh, just like mine when my patience had worn out. It seemed to say *How could you be so stupid?* in a way that was even harsher than the words would have been.

Oh, God, what have I done? I prayed in despair. My sweet-tempered ten-year-old was starting to sound like a shrew. And he'd learned it from me. Instead of running up the stairs to intervene, I walked up in shame.

When I came into the room, Tyler's eyes were open wide, his face pale. "It was an accident, Mommy. I'm really, really sorry. Can you fix it, Mommy? Please try."

I gave Tyler a hug and told him we would try to repair the damage. Then I told him to go back and play with his toys. I had more damage to repair than what had happened to the model.

Chase was standing in his room, his face flushed with anger. "I can't believe he broke it," he said. "And you're not even punishing him. That's so unfair!" he cried.

There it was again: my sense of injustice had found its way into my own son's heart. It was ugly and painful to see and even more devastating knowing that Chase had learned it straight from me.

I looked at the model carefully. "Chase, I think we can fix it with just a little glue," I said. He couldn't be calmed.

"It won't look right then," he said petulantly. "Tyler should have to buy me a new one. He wasn't watching where he was going. It's so unfair."

"Sit down, Chase," I said as I sat on his bed. He sat beside me stiffly, his face set in an angry scowl. "Tyler really didn't mean to do it," I said. "And he feels really bad. He loves you, and he wouldn't do anything to hurt your toys on purpose."

Chase wouldn't hear of it. "Oh yeah? I think he did it on purpose. He doesn't care about my things. I wish I didn't have a brother."

I was beginning to get angry myself. "Look, Chase, your brother and his feelings are a lot more important than your model. Do you understand that?" Chase nodded stubbornly. "Tyler apologized and I want you to tell him you forgive him. Then I'll fix the model for you."

"It's still unfair. I get punished when I ruin his things," Chase retorted, gathering steam for another assault.

"We try to be fair to both of you," I said, "but sometimes I know that I'm not fair to you," I added carefully. "I need to apologize to you. Remember when you spilled the soda in my car?" Chase nodded again, looking confused over my change of subject. "You said it was an accident, and you said you were sorry. But I didn't tell you I forgave you then. So now I need to ask you to forgive me."

Chase looked sideways at me, still irritated with his brother. "It's okay," he mumbled.

"No, it wasn't okay," I said. "I was being unfair, and you need to know that you are more important than my car, just like Tyler is more important than your model."

Chase was beginning to soften. He leaned against me, and I put my arm around him. "I love you, Chase. You're a good boy. I'm sorry that I've taught you a bad habit. It's not wrong to be angry, but it is wrong not to be willing to forgive.

"Do you remember the word 'grace'? You learned about it in Sunday school," I continued. Chase nodded miserably. "It means that God forgives us and still loves us even when we do something wrong—even when we do it on purpose. That's how much he loves us."

"God wants us to show grace to each other, too," I said. "He especially wants us to have a family that understands grace."

God forgives us and still loves us even when we do something wrong—even when we do it on purpose.

Chase's eyes were full of tears, and I realized that his anger was finally subsiding.

"I'm sorry that I'm not very good at showing grace to you sometimes," I said. "Can you help me be better at it?"

He nodded and hugged me.

"Are you ready to talk to Tyler now?" I asked.

"I guess," he said without much enthusiasm. I called Tyler and he came running in with his best eager-to-please expression.

"I'm really, really sorry, Chase," he said again.

"It's okay," Chase mumbled. "I forgive you."

Tyler came running over to where we sat and hugged us both. "I'm not happy about it," Chase said. "But it's called 'grace,' Tyler," he added, a touch of superiority in his voice.

"Grace?" Tyler asked perplexed. Then he shrugged his shoulders. "I like it!" he said happily as Chase and I laughed.

Thank you, Lord, I prayed silently. *I like it too.*

SEE WHAT YOU HAVE DONE

Something happened to me that day that Chase's model was broken. I was broken, too. So was Chase. Instead of being a good example of a mother, I was a good example of a sinner. God stopped me in my tracks and said, *See what you have done.* He said it gently, but it devastated me nevertheless. He showed me how bitterness and self-righteousness begin, and he showed it to me in the face of my own son, whom I love with all of my heart.

It would have been much easier to rush into the situation and play the referee. I could have remained in control with my children, and my dinner wouldn't have burned. But when God called me to turn toward the wind, he meant more than turning toward the tragedies in life. He was calling me to turn toward my own sin, to face the harsh truth about myself. No more running away, no more excuses. Although I was tempted to tell Chase that I was sorry I had yelled at him and to explain that I had been tired and impatient, I knew better than to offer the excuses that might have sounded acceptable before. Now I had eyes to see and ears to hear, and there was no turning back.

> *But when God called me to turn toward the wind,*
> *he meant more than turning toward the tragedies in life.*
> *He was calling me to turn toward my own sin,*
> *to face the harsh truth about myself.*

I had not just been tired. I had been sick. I had trod on my son's tender feelings and hardened them. I had rejected grace and exalted self-righteousness. And I had helped set in motion a habit that could take my son a lifetime to break.

SINS OF THE MOTHER

Children learn from their parents' examples. We've all heard it a hundred times, but until we see that familiar gesture or recognize the words in our own children, we still think that we can tell them what is right without living it out. From my own experience it seems that children are sponges for all bad habits, and the good habits seem to take twice as long to teach.

A few years ago, singer and songwriter Gloria Gaither edited a wonderful book called *What My Parents Did Right*. In it well-known, successful people recount stories of their parents and the good things they had taught them. Many of them attribute their success to a father or mother. It is an inspirational book for those of us still muddling through the parenting years.

There are so many reasons that I want to continue to change and grow. But one of the most compelling is to be the mother I need to be for my boys. I am already beginning to realize that I have little time with them and that their characters are forming almost more quickly than they outgrow their pants. My older son suddenly seems very responsible and self-directed. And my younger son, Mr. Live-in-the-Future, has already decided he wants to have five children – and has picked out their names. The other day he was fretting aloud about the possibility that he would marry a girl who wouldn't let him do the naming! It seems like only last week that I was teaching him to say his own name.

MIRACLES OF THE FATHER

In recent years we have learned about dysfunctional families and their high cost on children who grow up without good role models. The cycle seems to continue to the next generation unless there is professional help or divine intervention. Singer and writer Stormie Omartian tells her own story of childhood abuse in her autobiography *Stormie*. Although the terrible things that happened to her as a child due to her mother's mental illness were devastating, even more terrifying was that Stormie seemed to have an uncontrollable urge to hit her own baby once she became a mother. Through psychological and spiritual counseling, Stormie was able to control the responses that seemed programmed into her from childhood.

One day I was speaking to a women's group on juggling parenting and a working life, when a woman sitting at the back of the room stood up and interrupted my talk. "Excuse me," she said agitatedly. "These tips are all well and good, but it sounds like you had a happy childhood yourself. What about those of us from dysfunctional homes? What do you have to say to us, when all we can do is try to survive?"

The woman was obviously upset, and the crowd seemed to take a collective deep breath as they waited for me to respond. I honestly didn't know what to say. *Help!* I prayed quickly. "I *did* have a happy home," I admitted. "And yes, it is hard for me to identify with your struggles. But let me tell you the story of a woman who might have something in common with you." The words were coming quickly, and I realized that I was about to tell her a story I had heard before but had never repeated. I hoped it was divine inspiration, not lunacy that made me speak.

"There once was a family who lived on the prairies of South Dakota. They were immigrants, poor and getting poorer, as they tried to homestead in hopes of finding the American dream. But the winters were harsh, and there were too many children to feed. And then the mother discovered she was pregnant with yet another child. It was not good news.

"When the child was born, they simply called her Baby. They were too busy to name her and besides, it summed up their unhappiness about her existence. At least if she'd been a boy she might have grown up to help with the farming. But a girl was useless. With the harsh weather and the diseases that were around, she might die anyway, so better not to name her. By the time she was two, she was talking, walking, and appeared to be fairly healthy. One day she asked why she didn't have a name. In response, the mother suggested the other children find a name for her. They picked it off of the side of a boxcar as a train rolled by one day.

"As Leota grew up, she was strong, healthy, and bright. But school was a waste of time for a girl and besides, she was large for her age. She began to work, carrying sacks of grain on her back to the mill. Stooped over most of the day under the weight of the heavy bags, she grew up with a curved spine, resembling a hunchback.

"She wasn't much of a catch for the boys, and her family didn't have a decent dowry. So when Edwin came along and showed an interest in her, she didn't act too picky. He drank and had a bad temper, but he actually wanted to marry her. It was the first time she had been wanted by anyone.

"Leota and Edwin struggled to survive during the Depression. Leota bore four boys and had increasing physical problems with each delivery. Still, she got out of bed as soon as she could in order to help keep the family in food.

"Edwin's temper got him into fights regularly. He drank too much and began to bring his violent temper home. One day he picked up one of his boys and threw him through a plasterboard wall.

"Leota was miserable. She felt she would never escape the daily drudgery of her life. Then one Sunday she went to church and heard a simple message that changed her life: God loved her. It was hard for Leota to understand, but she felt it in her soul. He loved her and wanted to do something with her life. The next week she took her boys to church, too. They heard the same message and they, too, believed.

"Edwin was not very happy with the way the family disappeared on Sunday morning, but he was often sleeping off a hangover from Saturday night. But one Sunday he woke up early enough and decided to see what the rest of the family was so excited about. He went to church, too, and heard the same message. For Edwin the response was cataclysmic. It was no less dramatic than the cripple who stood up and walked. Edwin believed, and he stopped drinking. Cold turkey. He stopped fighting so much and tried to be a better father. He got involved in the church and became a deacon. He even helped build a new church.

> *Many people come from difficult backgrounds.*
> *But God can change us. We can become*
> *the beginning of a legacy of love.*

"Leota is now ninety-four years old. She is my grandmother, and one of the greatest women of faith I have ever known. Because of the changes in her life, she raised my father to be a kind and loving man. Because of her I had a happy home. Leota broke the chain of dysfunction in her family. So can you," I assured the woman.

Many people come from difficult backgrounds. But God can change us. We can become the beginning of a legacy of love. None of us is responsible for the past, but to some degree we are responsible for the future. Even if our childhood was as cruel as my grandmother's or as horrifying as Stormie's, we can give our children a better future.

We must face the pain of our own experience and get professional help if necessary. We must turn toward those experiences, not deny them. But then we have to believe in the God of change who wants to do a new thing in our lives and the lives of our children.

QUESTIONS FOR REFLECTION

1. What habits—bad and good—are your children learning from you?
2. How does your understanding of grace shape the way you discipline your children?
3. What are the difficulties from your own childhood that you still must overcome?
4. How can you leave the past behind and shape a better future for yourself and your family?

Chapter Thirteen

CELEBRATING CHANGE

The ringing of the phone startled me out of my stupor. I had stared at the empty computer screen for so long that I was almost hypnotized. "Hi! How's it going?" the familiar voice of my friend asked hopefully.

"It's not," I said in frustration. "Why did I ever say I would write this book?"

"Well, you did, and you will," Michelle said gently but firmly. "You really don't have a choice, so get to it."

She was right. My deadline was looming, and I had begun to feel sorry for myself. She knew me well enough to know that I was falling into a trap that would suck me further into inaction. Her words knocked me out of it, and I went back to work. The next day I called her. "Guess what? I wrote a chapter yesterday. I'd been working on it for a week, and I finally got it down. Thanks for not giving me too much sympathy."

Michelle is one of my friends who cares enough to tell me what I really need to hear. And she has the right to do it because she has also hung in there with me when solutions weren't as clear. She anguished with me over the struggles of a mutual friend and let me cry on her shoulder when a business decision became a disaster. She is also the person I can call when things go well, and I never have to worry that she will think I'm bragging. She genuinely shares my grief and my joy.

ENCOURAGE ONE ANOTHER DAILY

One day I was reading my Bible and came across the words of Paul in Philippians 1:3: "I thank my God every time I remember you." I was suddenly struck by how grateful I am to have a friend like Michelle. And I realized how much of the New Testament letters like Philippians dwell on the subject of how we are to relate to one another as changed people.

After having been battered by the world, wouldn't it be nice if we could come to church to be encouraged?

Over and over again, Paul and the other writers of the Epistles ask us to love and encourage one another. The early church was a group of believers who banded together to remind each other of the truth of the gospel, to encourage each other in their walk with God, and to take the word of God to others. Hebrews 3:13 tells us to "encourage one another daily." Paul writes in his letter to the Colossians, "My purpose is that they may be encouraged in heart and united in love, so that they may have the full riches of complete understanding" (Col. 2:2).

In many ways our modern churches have become so structured and organized that there is little time left to do the basic work of the church. And after having been battered by the world, wouldn't it be nice if we could come to church to be encouraged? Dr. David Jeremiah puts it this way in his book *Acts of Love*: "Encouragement is like a pebble thrown into water—while there is always an immediate impact, the ripples continue indefinitely. Paul spoke of this when he wrote to the Corinthians. 'I want you to know how blessed I am by the God of all encouragement who encourages us so that we in turn can encourage others with the encouragement whereby we ourselves have been encouraged'(2 Cor. 1:3–4, my paraphrase)."[1]

I believe that one of the reasons the churches of today are not as vital as they could be is because we do not take seriously the biblical mandate to encourage one another. We do not share our pain and our triumphs with others, we do not confront each other lovingly, we do not hold each other accountable, and we do not celebrate together when true change happens in our lives or in the lives of those we love. Although we sometimes have a relationship that satisfies these needs, we must find ways to make our churches more an embodiment of the New Testament principles. As people who are changed and continue to change, we need the help of others. As we are able to support one another, we, too, find the strength to stay true to our higher calling. A key way to do that is through accountability.

BE ACCOUNTABLE TO ONE ANOTHER

I grew up in a small town where everyone knew everyone else's business. At the grocery store we always saw people we recognized, my parents were friends with my classmates' parents, and when I rode my bike to school, I waved to the people I passed. One of the reasons I thought twice about disobeying my parents was that I was sure to get caught. In our town there was no place to hide. And, sure enough, by the time I came home from school, my mother would have already received a call from a friend telling her about the boy I kicked at recess. Or if I took a different route home, she knew all about it before I arrived. I was accountable not only to my parents but also to the many other people who made my business their business.

But if I really want to grow, I make myself accountable to others, asking them to keep me honest and to make my business their business.

As an adult I live in a large town, see my neighbors only occasionally, and come and go to the store without seeing anyone I recognize. I am accountable to my husband, my children, and the people in my office, but otherwise no one really knows where I go or what I do during the week. In fact, none of those people even knows if I binge on a donut, am rude to another person on the subway, or choose to ignore my phone calls and let them bounce into voice mail.

In those areas where my life needs work, I can get by with a great deal if I choose to. But if I really want to grow, I make myself accountable to others, asking them to keep me honest and to make my business their business. I need to keep myself open to their probing questions and be willing to give up some of my privacy.

My friend Becky called one day to chat. After the pleasantries she said, "So how's your Bible reading going?" She knew that I had decided to read through my Bible using a Bible reading guide.

"Fine," I said noncommittally. The truth was, I'd let too many other activities crowd into my life, and the dust was beginning to cover my Bible.

"Is it really?" she probed. "I've been praying for you to have the time to stick with it. It's really important, you know."

I admit that Becky's prodding was not all that comfortable at the time, but she was right. And realizing that she was taking the time to pray for me helped me get back on track. Becky's forceful questioning helped me keep to a discipline that has changed my life in many ways. The Bible puts it this way in Proverbs 27:6: "The kisses of an enemy may be profuse, but faithful are the wounds of a friend." A true friend wants the best for me, even when it isn't what I have chosen for myself.

> *A true friend wants the best for me, even when it isn't what I have chosen for myself.*

As I have moved along the path of change, I have also learned the importance of being accountable to those over whom I have authority or power. In my former company I asked those who worked closely with me to feel free to tell me when I was doing something they didn't think was right. I even set up review sessions so that we had a formal time for my review as well as theirs.

I try not to close my door or hide my actions from the people who work for me. I want to remember that my words are being heard by them and that I have asked them to hold me accountable. I have been fortunate to have employees who have taken this request seriously and have, from time to time, suggested that I am acting out of anger or have cut a corner I shouldn't have.

Leslie, who was my vice president in my publishing company, was an especially sensitive and committed friend who very gently pointed out things in my life from time to time. Besides being grateful for her professionally, I will always be indebted to her for the times she helped guide me back to the path I had strayed from.

As a mother, I have learned to ask my children to help me be a better mother. I am surprised by how often they offer me wise counsel. One year Tyler was very excited to learn about New Year's "revolutions." However, he missed the point and thought he got to make them for everyone else. "I've got your New Year's revolution," he told me, "never yell at Tyler, all year."

*As a mother, I have learned to ask my children
to help me be a better mother.*

We laughed at the idea, but later it was the basis for a more serious talk.

"Do I yell at you too much?" I asked Tyler in a quieter moment. He nodded his head enthusiastically.

"I try to yell at you only when I am afraid you are going to hurt yourself," I said. "But sometimes I yell because I'm tired and you and your brother have been fighting. Could you help me not yell so much?"

"Sure, Mom," he said with a grin and then threw his arms around me.

As the year progressed, I stopped from time to time to ask Tyler how I was doing. He helped me break my bad habit of losing my patience, and he and his brother did try harder "not to get yelled at."

CELEBRATE YOUR SUCCESSES

Every step from darkness to light is a miracle. Every movement from stubbornness to openness; from dependence on alcohol to sobriety; from anger to calm; from pride to humility. Because these miracles occur over time, the difficulty is for us to see them in ourselves. But when we see the evidence of God's work in others, it is cause for celebration.

I recently had dinner with my old friend Jack. We were discussing the high school graduation of his son and remarking on how well he had turned out. But then it was my turn to congratulate Jack on the miles he had come and on what a good father he had been despite the difficulty of his divorce and the years of child raising from a distance. We celebrated not only how well God had cared for his son, but also how well God had done his work in Jack. Because we have known each other for so many years, I saw the changes more easily than Jack saw them himself. And because we are good enough friends to be honest with each other, we could laugh together at ourselves as I reminded Jack—and he reminded me—of the times when we were young, confident, and in need of a good dose of humility. It was wonderful to celebrate after the years of pain and difficulty that had formed our characters and brought us to the point where we could both acknowledge that it had all been worth it.

When we see the evidence of God's work in others, it is cause for celebration.

Because Jack and I are old friends, we are able to encourage one another in a way that new friends can't. One day when I was despairing over a situation at work, Jack reminded me that it wasn't nearly as bad as a problem that had occurred ten years before. He was right. We both laughed at the situation from the past, and he helped me put my current "crisis" in perspective.

Having friends to celebrate with is a special gift. But you don't have to be close friends to encourage someone else. Maybe you know someone is on a diet, and you notice that her skirt is hanging more loosely. Congratulate her. Celebrate the victory with her. There is nothing more frustrating than making progress and not having anyone notice. And there is something even more exciting about having someone you hardly know take the time to compliment you.

I have a dear friend who suffers from depression. Whenever I call her and she is having a good day, I try to celebrate with her and encourage her. "You sound so great!" I told her the other day. Together we began to count the weeks since her last bout with depression. When we realized that she had gone for more than a month without a day of debilitating depression, we were both overjoyed. Before she had found a new therapist and had her medication changed, she was nearly suicidal at least once a week.

"It always seemed like as soon as I felt better I began to feel bad again," she said. "But now I have a sense that I can actually live a normal life. It almost seems possible that being depressed would be an exception, not the typical pattern."

For my friend, this change is revolutionary. It means that her life might really be different. Not only did we celebrate together, but I promised to pray that she will sense God's presence and that the medication will help her. I promised to expect the best with her, but I also promised to be there for her on any dark days.

My children have shown me the need for encouragement, too. When they are playing well together I tell them how happy I am to see them getting along. When Chase is patient with his little brother, I take him aside and tell him how proud I am of him. When Tyler asks permission before borrowing one of Chase's toys, I tell him that he is growing up and that he is being a good little brother. It takes more time to encourage rather than reprimand, but it has much more positive results.

I try to send congratulatory notes to people I know who get promotions or cards to those who say or write something that is meaningful to me. Sometimes a short note is a good way to celebrate with people and let them know they are highly regarded. Many days are full of criticism and setbacks. Everyone can use a boost and a reminder of something she has done right.

It takes more time to encourage rather than reprimand, but it has much more positive results.

I used to keep a file called "Letters to Read on a Bad Day." Whenever someone sent me a positive letter or a kind note, my secretary filed it away. There were days when she would quietly place the file on my desk after a particularly difficult meeting. I would sit back and read through the old notes and letters to help me recover some of my self-esteem. Those old letters always lifted my spirits and gave me the resolve to go forward. The kindness of the people who wrote to me over the years continued to help me time after time.

One of the wonderful by-products of celebrating change with someone else is the encouragement it provides for me. If God can work in someone else's life, surely he can work in mine. If God can help someone else's child through the terrible teens, surely he will be with my sons. If God can help a friend stop losing her temper uncontrollably, then surely he can help me become more patient, too.

God is at work in our lives. We need to celebrate this wonder together.

QUESTIONS FOR REFLECTION

1. Is there someone in your life to whom you are accountable?

2. Who are your closest friends? What do you gain from each of them? How can you help each of them?
3. Is there anyone to whom you are accountable at your workplace?
4. How can you encourage a family member today? How about a friend? A coworker?
5. When was the last time you dropped someone an encouraging note?
6. How can you help your church be a place of encouragement?

Chapter Fourteen

*S*OME THINGS NEVER CHANGE

A nyone who sails around Annapolis knows the "spider buoy," so named because it has a platform about fifteen feet square with great steel legs reaching out into the water. It is the home of several nests of osprey, the occasional duck, and a beacon light that cuts through foul weather, fog, and the darkest night.

No matter how lost a sailor feels, no matter how disoriented he becomes in fog or a storm, catching sight of the spider buoy lets him know that he is going to be all right. The beacon light promises a safe harbor and shelter from the storm.

As a novice sailor, I rarely venture far beyond the spider buoy. I enjoy looking at its huge structure. I marvel at how its legs are planted in the twenty-foot deep waters. I love to see the white-capped waves strike it and become harmless spray. I keep it in my view not only to help me navigate, but also to give me assurance. The spider buoy never moves.

The winds shift, the sun and moon disappear from my view, and even the shore is easily obstructed by fog. But as long as I am within a mile of the spider buoy, I know where I am headed.

I am learning to read charts and navigate by various markers. I have discovered where the channels are and am no longer in danger of running aground. But despite all of the other helps, nothing gives me peace of mind like the spider buoy.

I hope God doesn't mind the comparison, but I think he must be something like the spider buoy. Planted firm, his beacon light shines for all to see, beckoning us to a safe harbor. He never moves, he never changes.

IT'S ALL RELATIVE

We live in a world that worships relativism. Ask someone what is right or wrong and the answer is often "it depends...." As a generation that grew up with a healthy distrust of authority, those of us who are aging baby boomers have too often moved into cynicism and total disregard for authority. We have little respect for elected officials, police, and even the president.

Much of the reason we feel this way is that time and time again we have seen those we respect do things that are despicable. We have seen politicians win by cheating, lawyers bend the law to suit their aims, and presidents act unpresidential. "Who can we really trust?" is the question we ask.

The fact is there is only one person who doesn't let us down, and that is God. He is the one who never waivers, never needs to grow, and never changes. Hebrews 13:8 puts it simply: "Jesus Christ is the same yesterday and today and forever."

*There is only one person who doesn't let us down,
and that is God.*

Theologians call it the immutability of God. Both the Old and New Testaments contain such verses as "I the LORD do not change" (Mal. 3:6) and "Every good and perfect gift is from above, coming down from the Father of the heavenly lights, who does not change like shifting shadows" (James 1:17).

God is perfect. He cannot get better or worse. He always was and always will be. He is the one thing we can count on throughout this life and the one to come.

My limited human understanding has difficulty grasping this concept. When I was a child I thought my father was perfect. He knew everything, he seemed to be there whenever I needed him, and he was the center of everything that happened in our family. As I grew up I began to see that my father was a great and loving man, but he was not perfect. In fact, he was the first one to tell me so.

Over the years I have been fortunate to meet some great people and have interviewed them for different magazine profiles. None of them has been perfect either. In fact, the quality that stands out the most in my mind across all of the interviews I have done is that the truly great people were those who changed the most. They learned from their mistakes, changed their ways, and took a new path. None claimed to be perfect even then.

So what does it mean to us flawed humans that our Creator is truly perfect? What does it mean that he will never change while we are muddling through, making false starts, having growth spurts, and falling on our faces?

For me, the first realization is that I am not aiming at a moving target. The ideal that is set for me is not going to be something else next week. I can trust the fact that as I strive to become less like me and more like him, I am not giving up myself for a vague and shifting goal.

I worked for a man briefly who seemed to live life in a panic. "I need to give a speech over the weekend," he announced to me one Wednesday. "You write it and get it to me by 8:00 A.M. Friday."

It was a tough enough assignment, but it was made more difficult because I'd never really written a speech before. I wrote and rewrote the text, getting only a few hours of sleep between the time he gave me the assignment and Friday morning. When I delivered it to his office I asked his secretary where he was.

"He went out of town for a long weekend," she said. "His speech got canceled. I guess he forgot to tell you." She smiled sympathetically and added, "He's like that."

He *was* like that, I learned. Always changing his mind, never respecting others' schedules, calling on his employees to jump through hoops to do something that might or might not be important. He was the most frustrating boss I ever encountered, and my tenure with him did not last long. My respect for him was even more short-lived. I just couldn't trust him.

Some of us have a hard time trusting God because we have experienced so much pain and rejection in human relationships.

God can be trusted. He won't say, "Never mind." He will never jerk us around or let us down. And no matter how wonderful our parents were, or how perfect our spouse is, it is still difficult to imagine a relationship in which the other person is all we hoped he would be and more. Some of us have a hard time trusting God because we have experienced so much pain and rejection in human relationships that it is difficult to conceive of a relationship that has none of those negative qualities. But the more we get to know God, the more he supplies our needs—even before we know we have them—the more he is able to heal our wounds and make us able to trust.

The never-changingness of God is what brings us full circle; it is what gives us confidence that we are in good hands. He will continue to love us even when we sin, he will be there for us even when we stray, and he will want the best for us even when we are self-destructive. He will always want us to continue to move toward him and relate more closely to him. But he is ever patient and willing to wait. He wants to work in us and through us, but he needs our consent. He is not a God who imposes himself on unwilling subjects. He needs our cooperation.

"The immutability of God appears in its most perfect beauty when viewed against the mutability of men," observed A. W. Tozer. "In God no change is possible; in men change is impossible to escape. Neither the man is fixed nor his world, and he and it are in constant flux."

We are called by the God who never changes to be ever changing. It is one more heavenly paradox, another mystery in a life that is both temporal and eternal. For those who have set out on the voyage of change, there is no going back. As we move through the pain to the glory, we hear the wind whisper our name.

QUESTIONS FOR REFLECTION

1. What does it mean to you that God never changes?
2. How have the disappointing relationships in your life colored your ability to trust God?
3. What steps will you take today to turn toward the wind?

NOTES

CHAPTER 3: When Bad Things Happen

1. Henry Fairlie, "Fear of Living," *New Republic* (January 23, 1989): 14.

2. Christopher Morley, *Inward Ho!* quoted in Warren Wiersbe, *Why Us? When Bad Things Happen to God's People* (Old Tappan, N.J.: Revell, 1984), 51.

3. Wiersbe, *Why Us?* 51.

4. Philip Yancey, *Where Is God When It Hurts?* rev. ed. (Grand Rapids: Zondervan, 1990), 84–85.

CHAPTER 5: Two Hard Questions

1. Chris Thurman, "The Challenge of Change," *Today's Better Life* (Summer 1992): 39–42.

2. Martin Seligman, *What You Can Change and What You Can't* (New York: Knopf, 1994), 3.

3. The Twelve Steps are reprinted with permission of Alcoholics Anonymous World Services, Inc. Permission to reprint this material does not mean that A.A. has reviewed or approved the contents of this publication, nor that A.A. agrees with the views expressed herein. A.A. is a program of recovery from alcoholism *only*—use of the Twelve Steps in connection with programs and activities which are patterned after A.A., but which address other problems, does not imply otherwise.

CHAPTER 6: The Myth of Control

1. Larry Crabb, *Understanding People* (Grand Rapids: Zondervan, 1987), 186.

2. Ibid., 107.

3. Gerald Richardson and Judson Swihart, *Counseling in Times of Crisis* (Dallas: Word, 1987), 26.

CHAPTER 7: Reversal of Fortune

1. Lee Bandy, "Religion Changes 'Bad Boy' of Politics," *Orange County Register* (November 5, 1990).
2. Quoted in E. J. Dionne, Jr., "Recalling the Legend of Lee Atwater," *Washington Post* (April 5, 1991).
3. Henri Nouwen, *The Wounded Healer* (Garden City, N.Y.: Doubleday, 1979), 94.

CHAPTER 8: Facing the Good, the Bad, and the Ugly

1. Henri J. M. Nouwen, *Gracias!* (San Francisco: Harper & Row, 1983).
2. Thomas Merton, *Thoughts in Solitude* (New York: Farrar, Straus and Giroux, 1956).

CHAPTER 9: Living As A Changed Person

1. Virginia Stem Owens, *And the Trees Clap Their Hands* (Grand Rapids: Eerdmans, 1983).
2. Annie Dillard, *Teaching a Stone to Talk* (New York: Harper & Row, 1982).

CHAPTER 10: Traveling Light

1. Thomas R. Kelly, *A Testament of Devotion* (New York: Harper & Row, 1941).
2. Oswald Chambers, *My Utmost for His Highest*, 321.

CHAPTER 13: Celebrating Change

1. Dr. David Jeremiah, *Acts of Love* (Ventura, Calif.: Vision House, 1994).